FAMILYHOOD

Nurturing
the Values That Matter

DR. LEE SALK

SIMON & SCHUSTER
New York • London • Toronto
Sydney • Tokyo • Singapore

SIMON & SCHUSTER
Simon & Schuster Building
Rockefeller Center
1230 Avenue of the Americas
New York, New York 10020

Copyright © 1992 by
the Estate of Lee Salk
All rights reserved
including the right of reproduction
in whole or in part in any form.
SIMON & SCHUSTER and colophon are
registered trademarks of Simon & Schuster Inc.
Designed by Edith Fowler
Manufactured in the United States of America

10 9 8 7 6 5 4 3 2 1

Library of Congress Cataloging-in-Publication Data

Salk, Lee, date.
  Familyhood: nurturing the values that matter /
Lee Salk.
      p.   cm.
  Includes index.
    1. Family—United States.   2. Child rearing
—United States.
I. Title.
HQ536.S25   1992
306.85'0973—dc20   92-8195

ISBN 0-671-72936-5   CIP

Acknowledgments

I WOULD like to thank Mark Mellman and the Mellman & Lazarus organization for their assistance in making available to me the information from the Family Values Survey I refer to in this book. I would also like to thank Al Lowman for his enthusiastic belief that a book on American family values should be written, and his warm support to me and my family during my illness.

I want to extend my special thanks to Andrea Thompson for her great editorial skills and assistance in the organization and presentation of my thoughts.

*I dedicate this book to my wife, Mary Jane Salk,
whose strength, determination and love
turned a ghastly nightmare
into a beautiful sunrise.*

Contents

Introduction

THREE YEARS AGO, a comprehensive investigation of family and family values in America was commissioned by the Massachusetts Mutual Life Insurance Company. The study, conducted by Mellman & Lazarus, Inc., a Washington, D.C., research organization, attempted to find out just what people thought of when they talked about "family." From focus groups and a statistically valid survey of randomly selected adults, a valuable body of information was acquired, one that I believe will serve as a benchmark for future research concerning how Americans view the family and changes in its values.

I believe that every legislator, including the President, each governor, senator and congressman, and each corporate executive, human resources director, or anyone involved in setting government and business policy will be enlightened by this study. But just as important—and personally exciting to me as a psychologist and longtime advocate of the family—it makes clear the core strengths that empower us as parents struggling to raise children in complex and confusing times. And I welcome the opportunity to distill my years of experience in teaching and research, as a counselor to scores and scores of parents and children, and as a parent, in a book that talks about how we as individuals and as a society can promote the values that will make the next generation strong and that are, I am convinced, vital to our survival.

I abhor child-raising books that offer systems for controlling children's behavior or list ten ways to make them do their homework. They suggest a parenting-made-simple approach of recipes and gimmicks, but in fact, set up an adversarial and dishonest situation—here's how you can trick your child into getting into bed or learning math, into being nice to grandma or helping more around the house.

You don't need to trick your children. They are born with all the motivation and curiosity, all the eagerness to grow and willingness to please that you will ever need to establish a harmonious home and to raise secure young adults. Rather than imposing systems and schedules, what we as parents must do is work with our children and be honestly responsive to them within a family structure built around the central values of respect, responsibility and emotional support.

In the midst of my annual summer vacation in Maine, working on this book with my family all around, I experienced occasional difficulty in swallowing, minor episodes I felt only a hypochondriac might respond to. I would have sloughed the problem off if I hadn't, while discussing other matters, mentioned it to my physician. He insisted I be x-rayed, which led to an eventual diagnosis of cancer of the esophagus. One week I was a relatively healthy, happy person; the next I was in an operating room undergoing invasive and complicated surgery. My life was abruptly interrupted, beyond my control.

Following surgery, just about everything that could go wrong did. Gangrene developed in a section of my stomach, and most of it, and my esophagus, had to be removed. I developed pneumonia and infection around my lungs, in the pleural cavity, which required massive doses of antibiotics, causing kidney failure. Consequently, I underwent many courses of dialysis while still unconscious in the intensive care unit. I was on a respirator for five weeks and later underwent a tracheostomy to make breathing easier. Multiple cardiac arrhythmias required insertion of a pacemaker. At times, my systolic blood pressure reached levels approaching three hundred. Every system in my body was involved.

I spent six weeks in intensive care, in a state of isolation. My odds of surviving were extremely poor. Partly due to pain medications, my conscious mind was set adrift and I experienced unpleasant hallucinations. I felt I was in a helicopter, floating without control. There was silence around me, but somehow I heard people talking. I felt as if I were on the verge of disaster, as though the world were coming to an end. I had images of being off in another part of the earth, where I could communicate with no one. The respirator tube down my throat made speech impossible during my few moments of consciousness.

I remember seeing my family in flashes and reaching out to them, but I could never seem to touch them. In my hallucinations, I heard someone telling me, "Your blood pressure is going up. You have to stop this, Dr. Salk." I protested, saying, "I want to see my brother. I want to see my wife. I want to see my children. I've got to go." But I seemed to be restrained. In fact, I *was* restrained because I kept attempting to pull out the many tubes and arterial lines connected to my body. I was in a terrible state of physical and emotional confusion.

I recall being visited by doctors who asked me if I knew what day or month it was, or where I was or what had happened. I knew where I was, but not when it was; of course, I had no idea what had happened. I was unaware that I'd had a second surgery to remove my stomach, that I was now to be given nutrition through a permanent tube in my body, or that any food or liquid that I took by mouth would be collected in a plastic pouch attached to a small opening at the side of my throat.

I could feel my family's presence all the time and wanted to see them whenever I became conscious. It always hurt when I asked for them but was told by a nurse or attendant that they'd be back later. When I ultimately regained full consciousness I begged my family to get me out of the hospital. I couldn't understand why they weren't just taking me home immediately. I didn't know what month or day it was, or even if it was morning or night. Eventually, I came to understand that the cancer had been removed, but that my recovery would be long, hard and slow.

The full realization that I was no longer in control, no longer self-sufficient and independent, was terrifying. I was at the mercy of equipment and imposed routines. I felt I was going to be a terrible burden on my family.

But just the fact that I was alive and coming back to earth filled my family with great joy and happiness. They wanted me. They wanted me alive and well, and they made that clear. They gave me love and support and encouragement. They took over my care with no hesitation, no indication of disgust, no negative reactions. I am absolutely certain today that they were the primary factor in my recovery.

My wife, Mary Jane, was available day and night to help with feedings and medications. She told me repeatedly, "We'll make it. You're going to get well. You're looking terrific, you're looking great." It was always, "*We'll* make it." Even to this day, when I feel overwhelmed, she will tell me how amazing I am to come through this so well.

My daughter, Pia, flew in from the Midwest, where she lived at the time, and stayed with me throughout my hospitalization and beyond. She made milk shakes, all kinds of concoctions I craved for taste, and provided immeasurable comfort. She told me often and in various ways, "Daddy, you don't know how important you are to me. You mean everything."

Eric, my son, is a medical student at the hospital where I had my surgery. I saw him every morning when he came by just to touch me, kiss me, hold me.

My brother Jonas, whom the world knows for his work with polio and who is currently working on an AIDS vaccine, came from his home in California to help care for me. During times of good health we saw and spoke with each other frequently. Now Jonas was there night and day, monitoring everything the physicians did. Some of the thick tubes used to drain infected fluid out of my body were inserted without anesthesia; it was Jonas who on several occasions encouraged the physicians to please give me a breather during these excruciatingly painful procedures. When I finally began to turn the corner and improve, my wife tells me that Jonas, who is a sensitive man, took my hand and wept quietly.

Jonas's sons, all physicians, were in constant contact with their father, offering opinions and possible solutions to problems, and in contact with my wife even more frequently, consoling her. My brother Herman flew in from Palm Springs, California, to be with me. Later, when I improved and he was able to fulfill his commitment to teach in Thailand, he sent me frequent fax messages from remote locations, offering advice and encouragement. My sister-in-law, Françoise Gilot, was a mainstay for more than a month when I first came home. She came by many evenings, despite her own crowded schedule, to have dinner with my wife and then come and sit at my bedside for quiet talk. Nothing about my condition frightened her or put her off. She was very loyal and compassionate.

The months of recovery at home were difficult. Because I'd had two major surgical procedures, my chest was extraordinarily tight; every breath was painful. My blood pressure was low and when I so much as sat up it dropped and I became terrifyingly light-headed and weak. For a time, I had so little strength that I couldn't walk the few steps to the bathroom without oxygen—and I was fearful of even trying. None of this pain, however, touched that created by the tubes inserted into my intestine, held in place by stitches under my skin that pulled with every breath, every word I uttered. Through these tubes I received liquid nutrient every few hours, for me an extremely unpleasant procedure. More than once I asked myself, "Can I go on like this forever?"

I suffered constant, maddening thirst and an unbearable craving for sweets and couldn't get through the night without quantities of sugar-saturated tea or apple juice, all of which ran through my mouth and into the plastic ostomy pouch at my throat; emptying it constantly was another chore. Pain frequently woke me in the night, but I couldn't have pain medication at the time because the doctors feared side effects.

It seemed that there was nothing good left in life, nothing to live for. Except for family. Had I not had a family I probably would have been put in a nursing home. More important, my wish for survival would have been weaker. Indeed, I'm not sure I would have wanted to go on. But my wife, my children, my brothers were there for me, with encouragement, affection and constant care. Their love and need for me made me want to survive.

During the most critical period of my illness, the hospital personnel who cared for me were a kind of extended family. My surgeon is clearly proud of the intensive care staff and encourages me to go back and say hello. When I do, the staff is overjoyed to see me. I felt they were truly concerned about my life. I received wonderful cards and gifts from my family of friends. Some dear friends called my wife every single day, just to make sure that I was still alive. Former patients of mine who had heard about my illness wrote warm notes recalling help I had been able to give them in the past. They just wanted me to know that I had mattered to them.

As I write, it has been little more than a year since I experienced those first symptoms of illness. Today, although my body is somewhat changed, my strength has returned in full and I am once again teaching at the Cornell Medical Center, traveling across the country making speeches and appearing on radio and television to talk about the issues that face us as parents and families, the critical issues that have concerned me in my private practice, teaching, writing and speaking over a long professional life.

I have been told by the people who cared for me that my survival is amazing, a testament to phenomenal inner strength. I am a strong person, but beyond any doubt, the most powerful motivation to live comes from family. From the knowledge of being wanted, needed and loved.

Sandbar Island
Rockwood, Maine
August 1991

1

An Urge
for Family

*"The ideal family is getting hard
to come by. But I do think that
regardless of what's left of the
family—whether it's a father and
son, mother and child, or
whatever—you can still have a
lot of working together and
playing together. And teaching
the basic human values about
how to treat people and how to
be a good person. That's what it's
all about."**

FOOD, CLOTHING AND SHELTER, according to my second-grade
teacher, constituted the necessities of life. Those of us who enjoy
an abundance of these three know that to function as a civilized
person, to attain the best and brightest of life's treasures, we need
much more. We need to feel loved and to feel important in the life
of at least one other person. We need to feel acceptance and
respect from others for our uniqueness and to draw from that the
strength and courage to go about our business in the world. And
the one force that can make all that happen is the family.

Those Who Care

One summer day, while I was sitting on my porch at our
summer house in Maine, I witnessed a lively demonstration of the

---

* *Chapter quotes throughout are taken from the Mellman & Lazarus study focus groups.*

power of family. A swallow couple had decided that a little corner in the eaves above me was the ideal spot to build a nest. Instinct clearly told them that in this corner the winds and rains would be less treacherous, their nest would be safe, and they determinedly went about trying to scare me off, swooping down over and over and making threatening sounds. When I finally abandoned my porch to the swallows, they proceeded to build a nest, using mud, grass and feathers.

Over succeeding weeks, I watched the swallow parents protect the eggs, then take turns feeding the baby birds. When the adults determined that the time had come for the younger generation to set forth, they "launched" them from the nest with small pushes from beak and wing, then hovered nearby as the youngsters made their early tentative attempts to fly. What a clear-cut demonstration of the function of a family and of the drives all we living creatures have to reproduce ourselves, bolster one another and teach our young what we know.

The family is by far the most fundamental institution that human beings require; it is the key social unit within which we learn to love, come to terms with our aggressions, develop a conscience and acquire values.

A functioning family provides the individual with recognition for the successes and achievements that enhance self-worth. A baby for the first time accomplishes the very difficult task of grabbing her rattle, holding on to it and waving it in the air, and her parents smile and clap, tell her how clever she is and beam with pride. And thus a feeling of self-worth begins to grow in that baby, a feeling that will be enhanced and strengthened by continued recognition for all the subsequent small and big accomplishments in her life. From these experiences, in part, comes the strength and motivation to cope with life's problems later on and to become a productive member of society.

And we all know this intuitively. In study after study and survey after survey, there has been strong and overwhelming agreement that for the vast majority of us, the family constitutes our greatest support and resource system and our major source of pleasure and satisfaction in life. In my years of work in research and as a practicing psychologist, I have seen time and again that patients with strong and supportive families benefit more from treatment, recover faster and handle adversity more effectively than patients who are alienated from their families or are from nonfunctioning families.

Family values can help us transform the pressures and stresses of everyday life into challenges. And I'm convinced that strong family values enable us to come to terms with a rapidly changing world that can sometimes be overwhelming.

The 1990s Family: Issues of Change

But what *is* a family? Who makes it up? Where does it happen?

Traditionally, when we speak of family, we are talking about that group of people who generally live under one roof, who are related by blood, marriage or adoption and who love and support one another. We talk about two sets of grandparents, one set of parents and children. And when we think of the purpose of family, we think of the nurturance of children, the teaching and transmission of traditions and values, responsibility for one another's welfare, respect for one another's individuality.

Implied in these accepted notions of structure and function is the idea of cohesiveness, of "togetherness," the day-after-day communal life that in immediately evident ways or, less evidently, over the long haul provides reciprocal benefits to each member. But a quick tally of friends, neighbors and relatives demonstrates to each of us that the parameters of "family" have undergone a sea change within even a single generation.

As a result of the dramatic social forces and events of recent decades—increased sexual freedom, divorce and remarriage, out-of-wedlock births, a decline in fertility, and the rapid movement of mothers into the labor force—a range of new family structures has emerged. There are single-parent families; two-career parent families; blended or reconstituted families made up of couples who were married and divorced and who remarried, combining two sets of children under one roof; married or remarried couples with part-time or full-time stepchildren; and couples whose children are the products of adoption, in vivo, in vitro or surrogate processes. There are families consisting of homosexual couples without or with children who are biologically related to one partner or are adopted; divorced homosexual parents; childless families; and older divorced or married women who, for one reason or another, have assumed the parenting role to their children's children. It's a conglomerate of relationships that would have made your grandmother blanch.

We cannot—and never will—return to a society that offers its acceptance only to the family comprised of a husband as the financial supporter and a wife devoted solely to housewife and child-raising roles (although a significant portion of American families fit that model). Reality has it that these relationships, which are a departure from the "conventional" presumptions of a legal marriage, two parents and a heterosexual orientation, exist, have grown in number and have been increasingly accepted by society into the definition of "family." We have also seen legislative changes that have endowed some of these alternative lifestyles with the legal status of family and the rights therein that are recognized by the census, insurance policies, landlords and various others. In many other ways, of course, our institutions are still catching up to the realities of the life of the 1990s family.

But while much has changed, the core needs of human beings remain the same. People do not flourish in isolation. We need to love, to be touched. We need to be important to other people. We require one another. We require family.

Family Values: The Eight That Matter

The term "family values" is bandied about with great facility, and the presumption is that everybody is talking about the same thing. From a sociological perspective, values are ideals, standards, customs and beliefs that people of a given group or society regard with positive or negative feelings and that shape opinions and behavior. "American family values" have also frequently been identified in the discussions of particular religious or political factions. The assumption has been that if one considers himself "profamily," he accepts the views or tenets of these groups; not to do so is to be "antifamily."

In fact, until recently no one really knew what Americans perceived their values to be. With the completion of a comprehensive investigation of family and family values, we have an answer.

The Mellman & Lazarus study attempted to answer a number of questions:

What do people mean when they talk about family?
What are "family values" today and how important are they?
What are the threats to the American family?
What are people worrying about?
What do they feel good about?

First, what is a family? Earlier, I offered a definition of a family as a group of people who generally live under one roof; who are related by blood, marriage or adoption; and who provide love, care and emotional support for one another. According to the Mellman & Lazarus study, most Americans consider emotional or functional elements more important than structural or legal elements in defining the family. To the question "Which of the following comes closest to your definition of the family?" respondents replied in these percentages:

A group of people related by blood, marriage or adoption	22%
A group of people living in one household	3%
A group of people who love and care for each other	74%

Indeed, more than four out of five agreed with the statement, "My close friends are like a family to me." And almost one half said, "People at work are like a family to me."

These numbers make it sufficiently clear that we have come to accept alternative lifestyles within our definition of family. Perhaps in response to the indisputable fact that large numbers of traditional marriages and families have not survived the evolutionary challenges of modern life, the majority of Americans are focusing more on the interpersonal function of family than on the institution of family. In the eyes of the survey respondents, the two principal functions of family are as follows: family is the base for caring and nurturing; family is the place where values are taught and learned.

And Americans are very clear about what these values are. Participants were presented with a list of twenty-eight statements and asked to rank them in order of most to least important in response to the question, "How well does the term 'family value' describe each particular value?" Here are the leading eight:

- Providing emotional support to your family
- Respecting your parents
- Respecting other people for who they are
- Being responsible for your actions
- Being able to communicate your feelings to your family
- Having a happy marriage
- Respecting your children
- Respecting authority

The emotions associated with family ranked higher than mere states of being. People said, "Having a happy marriage," for example, mattered more than simply "Being married." "Respecting your children" was more important than "Having children." The quality of relationships, people are saying, means more than the simple existence of those relationships.

Furthermore, when asked to select from this same list of twenty-eight choices which were their most important *personal* values, people included in the survey picked the same eight. Clearly, Americans equate family values with personal values.

I'm tremendously excited and heartened by these findings. People are saying that family doesn't mean just the immediate relatives. Family means everyone who loves and cares for you, and whom you love and care for in return. And the most meaningful values within that caring group of people are respect, responsibility, and love and emotional support. "Respecting other people for who they are" is as much a family value as "Respecting your parents." And "Being responsible for your actions" is much more a family value than is "Having a good relationship with your extended family," another of the twenty-eight statements survey respondents considered.

As marriage becomes less a social obligation, an institution developed around a need for financial security and a requisite for child raising, and more a choice for companionship and love; as family takes on a startlingly broad meaning in public perception, Americans are reaching toward the deepest human needs to measure joy and satisfaction and to define standards of behavior. But while, according to the Mellman & Lazarus survey, people are pretty satisfied with their own family lives and list them as one of their top sources of pleasure, they are also deeply distressed about "the state of the family" in America. Matters, they seem to be saying, are going seriously wrong.

I'm O.K. . . . But I Think You're Not

At the heart of our nation's problems, people said, is the decline of the family; the quality of family life is pretty bad and it's going to get worse. Almost two in three Americans believe family values have gotten weaker, although an almost equal percentage say their own families did "pretty well" to "very well" in teaching them their values. Ten years from now, the majority of people said, the quality of family life is going to be even worse than it is today. And the great majority of respondents thought that most other people didn't place much importance on family at all, and were more interested in money and material things.

I believe such comments reflect two things: first, a perception that increasing crime, social ills, joblessness and homelessness can be traced to weakening family systems; and second, a vague but powerfully felt nostalgia for a time when life seemed safer, happier and more under control.

It's easy to exaggerate the appeal of "the good old days." In the 1950s, say, there may indeed have been more nuclear families, less pervasive problems of crime, delinquency and drug abuse than today. But behind the closed doors and within the "safe" structure of those families, life was far from perfect. The taboos and ignorance surrounding sexuality created confusion and anguish for many. For women who wished to work or assume roles in public life, options were limited. Fathers were often isolated from the lives of their growing children, both by the demands of being the family provider and by cultural norms that established the mother as the child-raiser. In many significant ways, "the good old days" did not offer a lifestyle we would seek to duplicate today, even if that were possible.

But, yes, without question, the weakened family is at the core of many of those ills that are undermining us as a civilized society. Over the last few decades, the idea of commitment to others and the obligations of parenthood—the ideals of family, parents and children—have been replaced by an ethos that has focused on self-fulfillment through individualism. As a country, we've made remarkable strides in offering legitimacy and protection to a range of "alternative" lifestyle preferences and structures and to individual rights. Certainly, equality and individual freedoms are to be desired. But we've paid a price. In our quest for freedom and our preoccupation with all kinds of "rights," we've corroded some of the very institutions we most rely on for our well-being, protection and dignity—and none with more devastating repercussions than the family.

While all people are profoundly affected by the weakened family, children are by far the hardest hit. These are the most vulnerable among us. These are the people who most desperately need to be loved and valued. Children who are not loved or valued are resentful, violent, destructive, poorly motivated to learn, have more serious emotional problems and are more vulnerable to drug abuse and suicide. To say that children who feel loved and valued by their families are stronger and far less vulnerable to these problems is not an oversimplification—research, clinical evidence and life experience tell us that is so.

A teenage boy and girl are found dead in the boy's car, leaving behind a note saying "no one understands"; a ten-year-old boy takes his father's rifle from its case and shoots and kills a neighbor child who had angered him; a youth strangles his girlfriend and then brings classmates to see her body in the woods. And journalists race to interview neighbors, teachers and relatives in an effort to understand and explain what contributed to such an appalling act. We read that the youngster was "a loner," "running wild," "preoccupied with guns and knives." The writer speculates on the negative influences of everything from unrestricted video game play to child abuse.

Behind all these descriptions and speculations is a core truth that mental health professionals and each of us recognize—that lack of love, early neglect, the absence of a functional family or carelessness or inattention in teaching the human values that make life precious can create a life destined for serious trouble. A law enforcement official in one of our large cities recently said that he estimates the number of jail cells that will be needed twenty years from now by the number of second graders he finds who are at risk at a given time.

This is a shocking statement. It tells us we are on an insane course of ignoring the solution to problems that are wreaking havoc in every city, town and village in America and generating barbaric behavior at an epidemic level that threatens to kill or maim us in the cross fire. This violence, as well as the staggering loss of human potential when we fail to intervene in young lives at risk, demand that we get serious, focus on relevant targets and mobilize our forces to accomplish the goal of strengthening functional families. Unless we do this, I believe we are seriously handicapped in transmitting the kind of values that we cherish, the values that enable us to be more cooperative and compassionate with other human beings and also serve to help restore civilized behavior and make us more conscious of our humanity.

New Beginnings

I believe we're ready to start taking those steps. Both individually and on a national policy level, Americans are recognizing the importance of family and articulating a sense of what we've lost and must regain. The Mellman & Lazarus study makes clear that if the "traditional" family is fading, Americans are forging a new definition of family, one based on the emotional human needs and responsibilities of a group of people who are sharing each other's lives. Within new frameworks we're looking for ways to get back the best of "the way we used to live"—a time when values were strong, when people were polite and respectful to one another, when spending time together and with our children was a cherished priority, when we were not desensitized to vulgar language, graffiti, intrusive noise, mounds of trash and casual violence.

The true power of family has always derived from day-to-day activities and expressions, the one hundred or one thousand small interactions by which family members tell each other I love you . . . You matter to me . . . Your feelings of well-being are important to me.

2
Beginning with Marriage

"My parents argued over stupid things all the time. In fact, my brother said, 'I wouldn't want a marriage like Mom and Dad's.' But even though they have these stupid arguments, they share so much together.
"Now, my mother for the past six or seven years has been in a wheelchair. She did for my father all those years; now he does the cleaning and he goes to the store and he's still there. That's what it's all about."

YEARS AGO, being married was in and of itself an important goal for both men and women. When I was a child, any woman who passed the age of twenty-one or twenty-two in an unmarried state was regarded with some pity, and by age thirty was regarded as an old maid or a prostitute. Today, of course, attitudes about marriage are dramatically different. Marriage is no longer a social obligation or the only institution ensuring economic security. Children are not necessary to carry out the work of the family. Unmarried persons are not considered peculiar or socially undesirable. People are marrying later in life and having fewer children, and many marriages do not last until death.

With these changing realities has come a heightened focus on the emotional benefits of being married, the sense that finding the right partner in life is the most promising path toward self-fulfillment and personal satisfaction. The Mellman & Lazarus study demonstrates that the intangible rewards of marriage matter more to people than the simple fact of being married. The value of being *happily* married was near the top of the list; the value of simply *being* married appeared much farther down. Similarly, while more than two-thirds of the people responding said they thought of marriage as a permanent commitment, not a state that should only last as long as it makes both people happy, it's clear from other responses that the psychic or emotional rewards of marriage carry real weight against the notion of permanent, institutionalized marriage. About a third of the respondents of all ages said that having an intimate loving relationship with another person was more important than actually being married.

People hold the idea of being happily committed in such high esteem that they're even willing to advertise themselves in personals ads in newspapers and magazines to find a "significant other." People want to get married. They want permanence in relationships. But the challenges to achieving that desired state are perhaps greater than ever.

The Impossible Dream . . . Or Just Bad Press?

One out of every two marriages ends in divorce, we read; the possibility of an enduring marriage is not good. But the idea that 50 percent of all marriages end in divorce comes from a spurious statistic. It's based on the ratio of the number of people who get divorced, say, in 1992, to the number of people marrying in that year. Such calculations ignore all the people who married before 1992, whose marriages are already in progress.

Considering the *total* number of marriages in the population compared to the number of divorces, the divorce rate comes down to around 12 percent. In other words, statistics really show marriage strongly in the lead. But that doesn't make for catchy headlines.

The media are often engaged in the process of distorting or changing our perceptions, and the media have not, overall, depicted many realistically happy marriages. Just as women in movies and TV shows frequently are portrayed in demeaning roles in which they're giddy or in need of rescue, so portrayals of marriages tend to alternate between the seriously conflicted or destructive—from petty sitcom bickering to *Fatal Attraction*—and the sunny, Cosbylike ideal.

People are fascinated by talk shows about extramarital affairs and bizarre relationships and by the relentlessly fun-seeking, glamorous life of carefree singles so often shown in the media. The idea conveyed is that youth, singlehood and beauty add up to freedom, and freedom is the requisite for a wonderful life. There's very little reinforcement of marriage as an institution. And little suggestion that happy marriages are not really Ozzie and Harriet or the Cosbys.

None of us is perfect, and imperfect people have imperfect relationships. Marriage requires accepting the other person for who he or she is and being able to live with that individual's shortcomings, failings and idiosyncrasies.

Patients have said to me, "I'm thrilled, I'm ecstatic! I'm getting married to the most wonderful person I've ever met!" I frequently ask, "What are the things you *don't* like about this person?" And when they tell me "Nothing!" I say, "Be careful, because there's always something wrong with the other person. And I have found that when you can learn to live with that issue and tolerate it and not be overwhelmed or make it the source of conflict, then you have the makings of a good marriage."

As two people become more profoundly acquainted, as they become more intimate, they begin to find disillusioning or disappointing things about each other. There has to be acceptance of the other person and his limitations and the certain self-knowledge that you can live comfortably with those limitations. You must ask yourself, "Do friendship and intimacy really drive our relationship? Can I live with this person happily in spite of the things I don't like about him or her?"

Sexual Connections

When we lived in a culture that didn't allow for sexual expression, many people had repressed sexual needs. It was unheard of, for example, for women to reveal that they enjoyed sex. Because sex was permitted only as the consummation of a marriage, the need to satisfy sexual drives led many into terrible marriages.

Passion is a wonderful thing, one of the profound pleasures of being human. But the passion that motivates an initial attraction to another is not sufficient basis for a marriage. When passion goes, the marriage may go too. Therapists who work with young couples commonly say that the intensely passionate stage of marriage—the time a couple is sexually ravenous for each other—rarely lasts beyond two years.

The sexual revolution unquestionably led to a lot of experimentation, which for some created the damaging illusion that sexual gratification was the ultimate goal of a relationship, but for many served as a liberating force. For some couples, getting to know each other sexually before marriage both dissipates sexual tensions and rules out any problems with that kind of compatibility. It may be easier to take the time to think clearly and ask, "Can I live with this person? Do we share values? Do our goals in life mesh? Are we good friends? Can we communicate well?"

I am not promoting promiscuity. I am suggesting that couples must see beyond the physical attraction and sexual arousal to explore their common basis for building a life. As M. Scott Peck writes in *The Road Less Traveled,* passion is a deception created by nature to bring people together. It's wonderful when it's there, but the real, hard work in developing a relationship comes after the passion abates, through the process of undertaking responsibilities and commitments, through recognizing and accepting that you and your spouse are two very different people sharing one life.

Growing Together

In my clinical work, I've talked with many patients about their marriages. I have been especially interested in marriages that have lasted twenty-five years or more. What are the factors that contributed to those successes? What enables a couple to stick together for the long haul? I've come away with a powerful impression of shared companionship: you've got your best friend at your side.

Certainly, many of these couples faced the same trials and tribulations, the pressures and stresses, as the people whose marriages ended in divorce. Every marriage faces bumps and problems. People have moods, a spouse is depressed or discouraged at times. But what I have seen in the most successful marriages is mutual respect, a recognition that one's partner is a distinct and separate person with aspirations, talents and skills that can enrich both lives . . . and that problems can be solved by a willingness to accept differences.

In the best marriages, emotional support is freely given and received. It means getting up in the morning and asking, "Did you sleep well? How are you feeling?" Offering affectionate gestures, kisses and hugs. Asking, "What are you up to today? What's going to be happening?" It means sharing funny moments, little jokes, conversation at the breakfast table. It means at times being giggly and childlike, at times being quiet and letting the other blow off steam. When two people feel they can share experiences and thoughts and feelings that they don't share with anyone else, intimacy and closeness are nurtured. Each partner, in words and gestures, conveys to the other: "You are more important to me than anyone else. I think about you. I will always try to understand you."

Within such an atmosphere of trust, there is very little that cannot be addressed. I believe strongly that couples must ask each other for the support they need. There's nothing wrong with saying, "Look, I need to talk to you. I'm getting a little worried about our financial situation. I wish it weren't so, but I think we have to cut back, be a little more careful for a while." Or, "I have a meeting at work today and I'm a little nervous about it. I'm not as prepared as I'd like to be." And, ideally, the partner's response will be: "I think you'll be fine. Your presentations usually go very well." Or, "I hear what you're saying. I understand your concern. Let's talk more tonight."

The most successful marital partners enhance each other's growth. Each respects the other's freedom, is not frightened by it, doesn't strive to possess the other's life or feel jealous of the other's accomplishments. And they don't feel they must do everything together. Divergent interests or friendships need not be a problem. People do things differently, communicate differently, because they're different people—and that can make life fascinating.

Each partner brings not only himself but a community of people—friends and relatives—into the marriage. Sometimes one partner in a marriage can help his or her spouse with old family

resentments or tensions. With one couple I counseled, the husband got along very well with his wife's family. But the wife had
unresolved problems with her mother and had, in fact, entered
therapy to work out her feelings of anger and frustration. As
much as she wanted to be close and affectionate with her mother,
she felt it would be compromising her values and compromising
some of the gains she'd made in the course of extricating herself
from a destructive dependent relationship.

Her husband acted as a buffer, making it possible for mother
and daughter to come together in a way that didn't ignore his
wife's concerns or dismiss her resentment. He encouraged her to
develop the relationship in small ways, saying, "Let's go visit
your mother this afternoon," or, "Why don't we send her some
of these chocolates? I know your mother likes this kind." Little
gestures that enhanced communication and made the mother
happy. He helped his wife maintain a valued relationship with her
mother without compromising what she had struggled to achieve
in her therapy.

All marriages change over time, if for no other reason than
that each partner is constantly changing and becoming someone
slightly different, intellectually, socially and emotionally. If the
change and the growth is in different directions, the partners have
to work together a little more determinedly to resolve stresses and
strains. Needless to say, flexibility, patience and understanding,
as well as a deep foundation of love and respect for one another,
can go a long way in making the relationship even more stable.

Some marriages can even tolerate "irreconcilable differences"
based on simple personality dissimilarities that need not lead to
crises. Some of the healthiest marriages of my acquaintance flourish because each partner accepts the other's different interests and
need for time and "space" to express them. Marriage doesn't
mean that each must constantly capitulate to the other or see
eye-to-eye on all issues. If respect exists for each other's individuality, differences can simply remain.

Having children obviously changes the nature of the marriage, starting with the amount of time and energy husband and
wife can devote to each other. Children can't be raised in spare
time. But having children also awakens in each couple ideas,
thoughts and feelings that neither partner even remotely expected
would occur. A lot of the old assumptions about what a family is

and how it works, carried over from each new parent's childhood, start to surface, requiring continuous adjustments. Does the father expect a son to be a good athlete, as he was? Does the mother want to do everything with her daughter differently from the way her own mother did it? Do fathers do laundry? Should mothers work? This surprising awakening is quite common, yet inevitably shocking to most married couples. It's as if their unspoken expectations about what life would be like after marriage is the fine print that goes unread in a contract; after children arrive, that print looms larger and larger.

As a marriage progresses into the child-raising years, the continuous process of adaptation and readaptation occurs at every turn. Small children wake up at night, leaving parents weak, tired and frequently distraught. As children grow and develop, their parents must make decisions about which toys to buy them, which television programs to let them watch, when to talk to them about sex, how to explain Grandma's Alzheimer's; they bring school conferences to attend and a myriad of moment-to-moment and day-to-day crises and actions that continuously influence the nature of a couple's relationship.

To varying degrees, children are incorporated into the parents' lives, influencing occupational choices and even where the family will live—are the schools good? are there other children nearby? The enormous emotional, social, physical and financial demands that become part of a marriage as a result of having children ultimately lead to yet another set of circumstances when children leave home. The emptying of the nest may seem like a welcome relief to many couples after enduring the pressure of getting their children through school and prepared for adult life, but some may discover that life is painfully quiet or slow without the day-to-day demands that were woven into their lives, particularly if the marriage was built largely around the children. When couples sacrifice self-development and the mutual nurturing interests that were strong before the advent of children, there is a greater feeling of emptiness, loneliness and difficulty in adapting.

While most parents are deeply devoted to their children, in light of the gargantuan changes those children create in a marriage it's hardly surprising that all parents have moments of strong ambivalence when they wonder what possessed them to have children in the first place.

Partners as Parents

When you have a good marriage, you have a partner to share your life—and, if you so choose, the wherewithal to bring children into the world, to raise them together, nurturing their individuality, helping them grow. For many people, having children affords the greatest feeling of purpose and immortality. But I don't think that all couples should have children.

Over the years, I've encouraged many couples I've seen in my practice not to have children—not because they're not capable but because it's clear from conversation that their primary goals in life lie elsewhere. A man or woman who is passionate about a profession, who has many demands on his or her time, may find it next to impossible to be a responsible parent. If children and family life will not be a couple's first priority, that couple's responsible course may be to choose not to have children. Such a choice, however, need not mean living a child-free life.

Couples who elect not to have children can make a concerted effort to be "weekend parents" for nieces and nephews, or for friends' or neighbors' children. They can "have" as many children as they want, be the Pied Piper in their apartment building or neighborhood, take their "child for a day" on special outings or work on projects together, and everyone benefits.

The child loves and is enriched by having other adults in her life, other sources of attention and appreciation. She's exposed to fresh ideas and activities, while her "regular" parents get precious free time to relax, enjoy each other or simply catch up on homework. And the childless couple reaps the benefit of the relationship—the affection, nurturing and fun—without having to worry about the emotional development, overall welfare and day-to-day care of the child. When Sunday night or Monday morning rolls around, the child returns to her loving parents.

Family life is a healthy life. It provides a kind of emotional, physical and psychological energy that has a positive effect on survival. And nothing gives greater faith or hope than watching the eagerness of young children learning, their fascination with what's going on around them. Nurturing that curiosity and excitement is tremendously gratifying. But a couple doesn't have to bear their own children to feel it.

Children really belong to the world; they don't belong to

their parents. Parents make a big commitment in assuming the responsibility for raising a child, but truly the child's life is his own. All of us should be deeply concerned as individuals for all our children and youth, because we will all suffer or benefit, whether we have children or not.

It is never too early to learn what having children and being a parent is all about. Some high schools are now offering courses in "marriage and child raising," urging teenagers to consider—through discussion groups and role-playing—what is really involved in assuming these adult responsibilities. This is all to the good, but I believe, in fact, that universal parenthood education should be started in elementary school. Youngsters must be made to understand the importance of making a commitment to the serious responsibilities of becoming a parent. Such a course, geared to a young child's level of understanding, would also discuss the alternative of *not* becoming a parent at all if either the man or the woman (or both) does not want to accept the primary responsibility of caring for the children. Girls and boys both need to consider seriously what it really means to be a parent.

3
Children and How They Grow

"Children have a lot of good ideas if you give them the chance. Just because you're older doesn't make you right. People are not listening to their children. The children want to talk, but the grown-ups don't want to hear it."

AT OUR HOUSE in Maine, we're often joined by friends who bring their young daughter for a visit. One day, when Skylar was a little under two, as her parents and the other grown-ups were sitting in the kitchen talking, she played happily with her Big Bird doll and her box of shaped plastic objects that fit into slots, then turned to the challenge of roasting pans, spatulas, kitchen canisters and several odd pots and pans. With glee, she picked up and dropped, pushed and pulled, pounded together and inspected these objects. As Skylar raced back and forth carrying a roasting pan almost as big as she, her sense of achievement visibly swelled. Clearly, she felt the master of this object. She carried it over her head and preened as if she were wearing a gorgeous hat. Then, as a finale, she gently placed the roasting pan on the floor and stepped into it. She looked down at her feet as she shuffled back and forth inside it, then looked over at her parents with an enormous satisfied grin. She proceeded to step gingerly in and out of the pan, very pleased with herself; each time she navigated the move from inside to outside the pan, her parents smiled, gave words of encouragement and applauded. The little girl beamed and laughed.

My young friend and her parents were, instinctively, giving a classic demonstration of what children need and how parents best meet those needs.

The Three Things Children Need

In my more than forty years of working with families and conducting research in family dynamics and the roots of human behavior, I have observed again and again a few truths. I have learned that all children—indeed, all people—need three certainties to feel healthy and positive about life.

First, a child needs to feel that she has options, that she maintains some control over her life. She needs to feel that she can do something to the world and the world will respond. In fact, stress, I believe, might be defined as a lack of options.

When young Skylar set out to learn what was good about a roasting pan, her parents let her experiment and explore, left to her the choice of whether to use the pan as a stepping block or wear it as a hat. No one said, "Here's a hat to wear . . ."

Numerous studies have shown that people who have choices are more highly motivated to work harder and even overcome daunting difficulties and pain. Burn victims in hospitals who are allowed to participate in their own care, such as by dressing their wounds, require less pain medication than those who are rendered helpless by having everything done for them. People want to help themselves. They become empowered in direct relation to the choices and options they perceive to be available.

The second thing that a child needs is to feel significant in the life of at least one other person. When Skylar's parents watched her manipulations of the roasting pan and indicated by their attention, their smiles and their words of encouragement that they enjoyed and admired her efforts, they were sending that small child a clear message: you and what you do are important to me.

Being ignored is devastating, one of the cruelest punishments possible. It leaves the child angry, depressed and frustrated. When people react negatively to the child, that arouses negative behavior. When the parent respects the child's efforts to express herself, encourages her explorations, applauds her small victories, from the first tentative baby steps on, the child thrives.

Third, a child needs to feel accepted because of his or her individuality. Skylar's activities were pure Skylar, her very own way of manipulating the things, and even the people, around her, demanding an audience and a little bit of applause, enjoying making a little noise and holding center stage. Each child deserves to be acknowledged and cherished for the qualities that make her unique, which can be hard to remember in a society that tends to encourage tolerance rather than welcome differences. Ideally, we should embrace others, and especially children, *because of*, rather than in spite of, their differences.

What Families Do Better Than Anyone

In the Mellman & Lazarus survey, Americans strongly identified what they perceived as the two basic functions of the family. First, the family provides the base for caring. People responded to words like "loving," "caring," "can always be counted on," and to the ideas of sharing and nurturing as most descriptive of their families. Said one, "I think of an ideal family as one in which there's love, mutual respect and communication. I don't care if there's one parent, two parents, etc. If those things are there, that's an ideal family."

The other primary function of family, they said, is to teach values. More than nine in ten agreed with the statement that "Family is the place where most basic values are instilled," and when respondents were asked to describe their own families, statements like "provided me with good ethical values" and "taught me responsibility," "taught me respect for authority" and "taught me discipline" tended to be at the top of the list. Indeed, families seem to be as much about teaching as they are about caring and closeness. Yet at the same time, today's parents seem a bit uncertain of their own power to influence their children's developing values. Children, said many of the respondents, need "better role models."

There's something about this talk of role models that confuses me. Who do we have in mind? Are we talking about Abraham Lincoln and George Washington? About athletes and rock stars? Children have always had heroes whom they worship, want to talk like and dress like, heroes whom they will change over the course of their development—from Ninja Turtles to Metallica, from Tiffany to Paula Abdul. Heroes are transitory figures in the child's life who offer examples of strength, style or skills that the child may find attractive, comforting or worthy of emulating. These transitory heroes are not really role models.

"Role model" jargon has been used in recent years to explain almost any problem. If children are tearing up schools, "they don't have positive role models." In fact, they are not receiving guidance for their behavior or incentives for wanting to emulate civilized behavior. They are not receiving love and respect and emotional support, and that must come first and foremost from the family.

The role model issue has become a cop-out, particularly for people who are having trouble making it. Some educators and political figures insist that African American, Hispanic and Native American children need schoolteachers of the same ethnic background, for example, so they will have positive role models. It is important for there to be teachers of all races and genders, but I'm not so sure we have to mirror the student population demographically, with the same percentage of teachers from various groups. What students need are good teachers and what the educational system needs are the teachers—black, white, Hispanic, male, female—who can most effectively transmit the content of the subject and display standards of behavior and personal excellence that children will learn from.

And what children most need are parents who are significant in their lives. Parents are their children's primary role models. Children learn from us and imitate our behavior, whether we like it or not. We learn to be humans by watching other humans behave, and children learn human values by watching their parents—how they talk to each other, how they handle moral dilemmas, how they take responsibility for their choices, how they treat their own parents, how honestly—or dishonestly—they deal with the facts of their own lives. Do they lie, are they intolerant, are they mean spirited, do they have compassion for themselves and others? Watching adult behavior is what animals do. A mother duck is not necessarily a heroine, but she is a role model. That's how her children learn.

The development of a set of values actually begins with the earliest basic lessons in cause and effect: when you do certain things, other things happen. Children learn from infancy on that their actions have consequences. And from their child's infancy on, a thousand times a day and without even realizing it, parents infuse their children with an understanding of what's important and what is not, what makes people angry or unhappy and what makes them glad, what makes them feel good about themselves or not so good.

I've often used the example of a toddler sitting in a high chair who is given a cup of milk to drink. As he's drinking the milk, a fortuitous twist of the wrist sends it all over the floor. He is amazed at what he can do, and amazed that Dad, who was standing there with a smile on his face, is now down on all fours mopping up the milk. In place of a smile, he's got a scowl. And the floor that was green is now white. This is an absolutely phenomenal feat in a young child's eyes. It's the beginning of learning that he can do things to the environment, and the environment responds.

The next concept for the toddler to learn is that it's not a good idea to do that trick again. Dad gives the child another small cup of milk and says, "No. Not on the floor. This is for you to drink." Now, any red-blooded child will look his father straight in the face and pour the milk, with great deliberation, on the floor. And if his action elicits the same reaction, he smiles. He thinks, "Wow! I did it again. And I'm getting the same results!" He has control over his world.

The parent continues to teach, showing the child that while he can't drop the milk, he *can* drop something else. Children, in fact, are fascinated with the idea of gravity, the realization that they can release something and it goes down—it doesn't go up. Dad now takes a napkin or a piece of paper, crumples it up and gives it to his son, smiling and acknowledging that it's all right to drop this over the edge. And he does, while drinking his milk.

Cause-and-effect has been taught and learned, and social skills as well: some behaviors are acceptable and some are not. While they discover there are things they can do, children must also be made to realize that there are other things they should not do. And if they repeat those things, you will be annoyed and angry. As they get older, children learn that certain actions or words will elicit a punishment or consequence, such as a reprimand in an angry tone of voice. There's nothing wrong with this. Ignoring a child's destructive or socially unacceptable act, even such a mild one as the spilled milk, does a disservice to the child. The parent is saying, in effect, "It's okay for you to do this if you feel like it," or, worse, "I don't really care what you do." Either message not only discourages the child from thinking before he acts, it also confuses him. The child wants to feel that when he does something, it creates a response, even if he doesn't especially like the reaction.

Play as the Child's Work

A child starts learning values when a caring adult who loves her and whom she loves responds to what she does. It's as simple as that. A mother babbles baby talk to her infant—"You are the *most* best, *most* wonderful, *most* spectacular baby anybody has ever seen in the whole world . . ." A father engages his baby in a "serious" discussion—"I can see that you like grass better than I do, so when you get a little older, I'm going to show you how to be a champion lawn mower." It hardly matters what the words are. Even the tiniest infants listen to vocal rhythms, study facial expressions and know that someone is paying attention. A parent's responsiveness, in talks and hugs and expressions of fun and joy, tells the child that she is just fine. A confident, happy child is a child who plays. And playing is one of the main ways she learns everything from mathematics to physics to aesthetics. Play is the work of childhood.

To an adult, play activity can seem benign. We enjoy seeing them have fun and being occupied, but it's "only" play, and it's easy for a parent, eager to keep to a schedule and get through everything that needs to be done, to forget that a child who is playing is a child at work. A mother watches her son starting out to build a bridge with his Legos, then looks at her watch and notices it's 5:30. "Whoops, bath time," she says, and scoops her boy up for his evening cleanup.

It's critical for a child not to feel, "Every time I start something and I get involved with it, I get interrupted." Interruptions and interference are terribly frustrating. If they happen repeatedly, the child will be reluctant to start projects. He is also deprived of the opportunity to learn to undertake a task that may take time and perseverance. A bath can always wait.

Perhaps he has almost finished his bridge or house of blocks and as he puts the last piece on the top the whole structure falls down. Terribly frustrated, he cries and starts throwing blocks all over. This is a time for Mom to say, "It's all right. This kind of thing happens sometimes. Let's try to do this again." With a little emotional support and a bit of construction assistance, he is led to build a bigger and better house of blocks. And as the child's parent smiles and offers a hug, she reinforces his sense of pride and conveys the message, "You see, if you stick with it, you can do it. And don't you feel good about yourself?"

For a very young child, the richest play happens in an environment filled with lots of things—pots and pans and empty shoe boxes and pieces of string, as well as toys—that he can explore, choose from, and make something happen to. And nearby, a caring parent or other adult with the awareness that what the child is up to is very important indeed, the patience to let the child proceed at his own pace and the willingness to be a play partner when the occasion demands. I don't believe in play groups for children under three. Two-year-olds will imitate the behavior of other two-year-olds, which can mean they learn mayhem. "Early socialization" is not really being taught or learned in play groups. At this age, the small child needs a lot of one-to-one interaction with a sensible, warm, loving adult, not a group.

There's a very different feeling between the parent who teaches the child and the parent who provides the opportunity for learning, not unlike the comparison between run-of-the-mill and outstanding teachers in our educational system. A parent need not even make a conscious effort to teach. In the best kind of play between a mother and her toddler, Mom isn't "teaching," she's providing opportunities for discovery and for her child to use his own resources; discovery and learning happen as if by magic. And the child feels wonderful about what he's accomplished, which leads him to want to try more and more, a kind of natural exploration that's far less likely to happen if the youngster is following a "learning program" and someone else's schedule.

When a Child Is Ignored

Children know when they're being brushed off or belittled. Every child has been in the presence of relatives or family friends who make mindlessly hurtful or belittling remarks about the child, or make fun of him in grown-up-to-grown-up talk in front of the child. Young children may not understand sarcastic humor or clever remarks that go over their heads, but when an adult talks to a child in these ways in an effort to amuse or impress the adults present, that child feels very well what's going on.

But often, loving, caring parents, too, brush their child aside and ignore her need for attention. Especially after a tiring day, Mom or Dad may be tempted to ignore a child who keeps interrupting. A little girl is trying to talk to her dad, who wants only to be left alone to read his paper. The child becomes whiny, trying harder to get some kind of acknowledgment, until Dad finally says, with irritation, "What do you want?!" It's a very human response, but it's a damaging one. It seems a message that children's interests and feelings don't matter. And it makes the child work even harder, in ever more annoying ways, to get her parents' attention.

Most parents want to treat their children with respect. In the Mellman & Lazarus survey, respecting one's children was among the eight family values that Americans said they considered most vital and was also listed as one of the most meaningful personal values, almost as important to people as respecting their own parents and respecting other people for who they are. "People are not listening to their children," commented one respondent. "You have to respect your children's opinions . . . and not always be right but give them their chance. Just because you're older, doesn't make you right." But in the rush of daily life and in the face of a young child's often ill-timed demands or emotional neediness, it is often difficult to honor that instinctive desire to respect our children.

It's so important to remember that simply paying attention shows respect, and that there are ways to deflect a child's "Right now!" needs without damaging her feelings or ignoring the parent's wishes. When my son was little and demanded my attention while I was having a conversation or in the middle of something, I would try to say, "Excuse me, Eric, could you wait just a minute until I finish this? Then I'll talk to you." And I would stick to that promise.

When busy or distracted parents more or less ignore a child's efforts to get attention, or to explore or try something new, and when they don't respond when the child does something right or something wrong, the child becomes depressed. He develops "learned helplessness," a subtle "What's the use?" feeling. If over time his efforts continue to be unacknowledged, he stops caring, stops trying and may start to withdraw, because being ignored is painful. Or he may learn to play by himself, conjuring up a playmate or acting out fantasies, which is actually a positive effort to deal with the pain of an environment that doesn't stimulate or reward. Through fantasy and make-believe, he creates a more gratifying world. Being ignored can even effect a child's body. Neglected children are more prone to illnesses. Happy, motivated, acknowledged children are healthier children.

So many parents worry about "spoiling" their children, starting even in the child's infancy, and see this early spoiling as the precursor to later disciplinary problems. Even today, when we are generally better enlightened about an infant's needs and development, I hear both parents and trained nurses state, "When Baby cries, don't rush to pick him up. Don't spoil him." If I had my way, every person in America would pick up every crying baby and we would banish once and for all the notion of spoiling a little child. A baby's cry is distressing by Nature's design; it forces a parent to respond to Baby's needs. Infants under the age of nine or ten months are utterly dependent, completely incapable of satisfying their own wants and absolutely unable to put off gratification without a sense of frustration. Babies require the cooperation of adults to survive and have needs satisfied. The child who has enjoyed a gratifying life during early infancy feels safe in the world and believes he has the power to shape events.

This belief is really the bedrock of a healthily disciplined child and young adult.

There's nothing wrong or childish about needing recognition; we all want our efforts to be noticed and appreciated. Years ago, a study was conducted of assembly line behavior in a car factory. Films taken without the workers' knowledge revealed one man who every so often picked up a hammer and smashed a fender on a car passing along the line. Researchers noticed that he had a smile on his face and a vigorous stance to his body each time he hammered. When he was interviewed afterward, he explained his actions: "At least I felt I was doing something special. I could say, 'Look, I did that,' at the end of the day."

That factory worker was not unlike a child who would rather misbehave and be punished than be ignored. Getting scolded feels better than no response at all. I'm uncomfortable when parents say of a child, "Oh, he's only doing that for attention. Just ignore him." Almost always, when a child "acts up," does irritating things or repeatedly asks questions, there's a reason. And the reason usually is, he needs the attention, he's feeling neglected.

Older children need a parent's attention just as much as when they were little, although you won't know it by tugs on the sleeve or whiny voices demanding your time. During the teen years, when a youngster typically turns inward, she still wants to feel that her parents are right there and paying attention, even when large areas of her thoughts and feelings become off limits to a parent's curiosity and when peer-group power is in the ascendancy.

So many parents who earnestly want to do well by their children, learn "how to communicate" and guide them safely into a productive young adulthood overlook one of the simplest, nicest ways to show that attention is being paid—the small, spontaneous gesture that lets the child know he's important to someone. Why not pick your daughter up after school, without preplanning, and spend time shopping or stopping for coffee and a Coke? If you think she would be uncomfortable when you show up unexpectedly, make a date. Put flowers in her room, or make sweet potatoes the special way she likes them. Call home from the office on an afternoon to say, "I just saw a magazine article that would interest you." All small ways to express the fact that you have been thinking about her. And she will be so pleased.

The Discipline Problem: Structure vs. Punishment

The Mellman & Lazarus researchers got an earful about parents who fail to discipline their children. The overwhelming majority of Americans responding to the survey agreed with the view that "Parents today are too lenient and permissive with their children." One father talked about the discipline problem and about the differences between "then" and "now." "You were taught at home that when you were spoken to, you did it. You knew it wasn't asked a second time. And you knew to say 'Yes, sir' or 'Yes, m'am' and 'No, m'am' to your elders. You better not step out of line . . . It didn't kill us. In fact, it taught us respect. It taught us that you don't do that next time."

Many couples raising their own children struggle with that perception and with the sharp sense that they somehow "minded" their own parents more willingly, readily or inevitably than their children do them. "I would *never* have talked to my mother the way Katie does to me," says a single woman raising a bright, funny, combative, endearing ten-year-old. She wonders how to get from "back then" to now, how to foster the kind of open, interactional, good-humored relationship she enjoys with her daughter *and* have Katie do what she says.

Most parents would agree, I think, that in some ways they have better, stronger, freer relationships with their children than they did with their parents. In general, we talk to our children more—and more openly—than our parents talked to us (and probably they talked to us more than *their* parents did to them). Father is not so typically the distant authority figure that he was a generation or two ago. Children do grow up faster in our modern society, know more and, appropriately, have more to say.

So how do we discipline our children today?

What parents may mean when they describe a lack of discipline is really a lack of structure. To live in the world requires understanding and acceptance of certain rules and regulations. To live in a family requires understanding that group's rules and regulations. It is a parent's responsibility to convey that sense of structure to the child. What discipline is *not* is punishment.

All those rules, regulations and expectations that regulate a child's conduct constitute discipline. Teaching your child to follow them helps him adjust to the world, understand the way the world works, and become aware of other people's rights and what he should do to respect them. But more than this, and most important, disciplining your child tells him that you are concerned about his behavior and you care about how he acts; in other words, you love him. Most children will tell you that when grown-ups let you do anything you want, it's scary. And if they could articulate their feelings, they would say, "My parents don't care what I do, and that means they don't love me." Discipline and love are on a continuum.

I sometimes describe discipline as a set of rules of behavior that are like the rules of a game. Consistency in enforcing the rules is important to maintain "the game," as any child who changes the rules of the game to suit himself finds out; the game stops because no one else will play. In fact, children enjoy playing games that have rules, a very strong indication that children not only like rules, but seek them out.

If a parent is *inconsistent* about what rules she expects will be followed, the child becomes anxious. The mother is unpredictable, the child begins to feel unprotected and confused, as if nobody cares about him, and then, most likely, he misbehaves—not to make his mother angry or unhappy, but to search out her rules and test them sufficiently to be sure that he will be protected by them. He can relax only when he feels his parent will be strong enough and concerned enough to show him, through her consistency, that she cares.

Imposing structure on family life and on children's behavior is more than establishing a list of don'ts and have-tos. It also means taking charge and organizing the day so that the child knows what to expect. A father might say, "Here's what we're going to do. We'll have dinner together at six o'clock. After that, you'll do your homework and I'll check it, and then let's sit down and play a game together." Children love the idea that things are planned and organized, even if they object on occasion when they reach those stages in development where they're trying to assert themselves and establish their independence.

If we think of discipline in terms of structure and love, it becomes not so difficult after all to see how we can raise "well-disciplined" children who also feel sufficiently empowered to challenge us and disagree with us on the way to becoming independent.

Of course, when rules are broken, the violator should pay a price. In the interests of promoting a child's freedom, the most concerned, well-intentioned parents sometimes prevent their children from learning that they have to pay the consequences of what they do. That's a lesson all children must learn, from the toddler who is experimenting with what happens when he pulls the dog's tail, to the teenager who takes the family car without permission. But the price must be not out of proportion to or out of context with the "crime."

Depriving a child of playing in a very important baseball game that he has greatly anticipated, or grounding him for a month because he didn't clean his junk up off the floor when told to is ridiculous. Picking up junk and being grounded or kept from playing in an important ball game are unrelated actions— one in no way naturally follows from the other, as consequences do in real life. It would be more appropriate perhaps to stand over the child while he cleans up his junk. The punishment should be both qualitatively and quantitatively equivalent to the child's misdeed.

When the punishment is inappropriately severe, the child may see it simply as a matter of grown-ups being mean, thereby losing sight of what he did to provoke the punishment. In that case, he is not learning the kind of behavior the grown-up is trying to teach. I remember a child who, because he pushed a girl in class, was made to write "I will not push a girl" five hundred times. In talking to him, it became apparent that this punishment would not alter his behavior toward girls, but *would* alter his behavior toward his teacher. The next time he felt like pushing girls he would make sure the teacher wasn't looking. The severity of the punishment is what determines whether a child incorporates a sense of guilt and a sense of responsibility, which is the aim, or focuses instead on the unjustness of the punisher. The child should feel "I've done something wrong, but now it's within my power to do something to make up for it. And I don't think I'll do that again."

With older children, a parent can sometimes negotiate a punishment. She can say, "Okay, you know you violated this rule and I have to punish you in some way. What do you think is a fair punishment?" Children actually tend to be more punitive than parents would be. I remember one child who suggested, "Don't feed me for a month." I said, "We can't do that." He said, "Then don't feed me for two weeks."

When the child helps determine his punishment, he's more likely to internalize the rules the grown-ups want him to follow. He's also less likely to complain about or try to get out of the punishment later, and he sees the parent as a model in terms of compassion, responsibility and consistency.

Can a Family Be a Democracy?

A colleague of mine in the area of group dynamics believed absolutely that his family—which included his wife and two children—should be run as a democracy, with each member having an equal say in family decisions. They carefully discussed everything, from where to go to dinner, to appropriate bedtimes for the children. They even voted. Invariably, the two children assumed one position, the parents another, which usually led to a great deal of further discussion and many painfully contorted compromises. The system, cumbersome as it was, worked after a fashion, until a third child came along. When this youngest family member first learned to say yes and no, his siblings immediately lobbied for his vote. The three children outvoted the two adults, and havoc reigned. The democracy collapsed.

A family needs an authority figure (or two). It must be run in an autocratic way, but it must also be an autocracy with a soul and a heart and with respect for its constituents. As parents, we have all heard ourselves say on occasion, "You'll do it because I'm your mother and I say you have to do it!" The occasional dictatorial outburst is only human and does no harm. But as a parental modus operandi, it not only doesn't work over the long haul, it doesn't instill and encourage the values children need.

Someone has to be in charge and that someone should never be the child, although ideally she will feel her opinions have weight and count. Children feel important and respected when they participate in grown-up decisions. If the parents are planning some serious shopping, for example, they might say to the children, "We're going to buy some new furniture for the living room and we want you to come along and give us your opinions.

We'll try to find something we all agree on, but if we don't, Mom and I will make the final choice."

And the Greatest Is Love

In my work in residential treatment settings and in my clinical work through the years, I have been most intrigued by those people who turned out better than, by all indications, they should have—individuals who survived appallingly dysfunctional families, who navigated a path through terrible adversity and prevailed in the face of circumstances that predictably should have led them to jail or some serious psychopathology. What happened?

In almost every case someone significant and responsive was present in that individual's early life. Perhaps a grandmother whose fierce love was the one positive emotion; a social worker who went beyond doing a job to give the child the sense that someone cared; a teacher who encouraged and praised and pushed the child to yield his best efforts; a neighbor who wasn't reluctant to intervene to fill the empty spaces.

I've learned that the need for "a loving other" is so powerful that a child who does not feel the presence of that loving person in his life will often try to will one into existence.

Years ago when I was working under the supervision of Dr. Selma Fraiberg, a wonderful woman and the author of the classic book about early childhood development, *The Magic Years*, I got to know a ten-year-old boy who was attending a summer camp of the residential treatment center at the University of Michigan. As we sat around the campfire one evening, he told the other children, "My mom is great. She's a great cook, too. She comes home and makes barrels of cookies and invites all my friends and all the kids in the neighborhood over. And they all come in and eat all the cookies they want. Everybody thinks my mom's terrific."

I was aware that in fact the child's mother was a prostitute who frequented a bar where the boy had to go meet her after school. There he watched his mother's solicitations. He sometimes played the piano to amuse himself until it was time to return home with his mother and her evening's customer. His father was not a part of his life. This youngster was a case study in neglect. And out of his need, he created in his mind the idealized mother whom he could find loving and gratifying.

Happily, that boy was not beyond hope. He was relating to something positive, if only an image of love, and he did have a grandmother who cared what happened to him.

A child grows best when he is well loved, and it is only through love that a parent summons the wit, wisdom and resiliency to nurture and guide the child through his ever more challenging stages of development. My colleague Urie Bronfenbrenner has written eloquently about family dynamics and the needs of children. He recently outlined a series of propositions defining the optimum requirements for the growing child. First among them:

> In order to develop—intellectually, emotionally, socially and morally—a child requires participation in progressively more complex reciprocal activity, on a regular basis over an extended period in the child's life, with one or more persons with whom the child develops a strong, mutual, irrational emotional attachment and who is committed to the child's well-being and development, preferably for life.

That "progressively more complex, reciprocal activity" he likens to a years-long Ping-Pong game that starts slowly, becomes faster and more complex as the players grow, change, adapt to and challenge each other. Says Bronfenbrenner, "In sum, it can be said that human development occurs in the context of an escalating psychological Ping-Pong game between two people who are crazy about each other."

4
Home Time

"I have the best memories of my childhood. When I was younger, every night my mom would come in after I was put to bed, and she'd kiss me good night. And she'd sit there for a couple of minutes and we'd talk a little and she would leave. Then my dad would come in and kiss me and we'd talk a little and he'd leave. And I used to look forward to their coming into my room for those few minutes. I remember that like it was yesterday."

WHEN I THINK of my childhood, I always have a clear sense of the overriding principles that motivated my parents' decisions and actions, which in turn shaped so much of my brothers' and my goals and actions during our growing-up years. Education, my parents let us know, was terribly important. I hear my mother's words: "People can take everything you have away from you, but they can never take away your knowledge." Her admonition to "always give something of yours back to someone who has less than we do." Her insistence that we save leftover bread for the birds in the park or give some coins to a needy person on the street.

But just as vividly I remember isolated, happy moments and small family rituals—my mother taking us to Horn & Hardart's for a spur-of-the-moment baked beans lunch on a day when school was closed because of a snowstorm, my father's habit of reading a newspaper article aloud while we waited for dinner. In large part, those times were what gave my brothers and me the greatest measure of security and contentment, made us feel surrounded by and connected to the people we loved.

That feeling of nurturing envelopment, of loving connectedness, is, I believe, what the Mellman & Lazarus respondents were identifying when they said "providing emotional support" was the key, single, most important family value in their lives. They described that support as guidance, as communication, as the root of self-confidence, as "love no matter what." Clearly, even amid the myriad configurations of modern-day families and in the face of too much to do and too little time together, people still look to family for their main emotional sustenance. We need to remember that there are many ways each day to enhance those good feelings, small demonstrations of support that give as vital a sense of emotional connectedness as do the larger rituals of family life.

What Children Remember

As a society, we feel deeply pressured by lack of time. As parents, we are bombarded with advice on the relative merits of quality versus quantity of time spent with our children. During the 1970s and 1980s, because of both the changing economy and women's changing career ambitions, many American homes became two-paycheck households. In the 1990s, even if a woman wanted to work full time in the home, many families would find getting by on one paycheck virtually impossible. The great increase in two-career families and single-parent families has meant that most of us have less family time than we'd like. Parents feel terribly guilty about shortchanging their children, and, consequently, themselves. The great majority of Americans responding to the Mellman & Lazarus survey agreed that families seem to spend less time together than they did thirty years ago. Almost half were unhappy about the amount of time they spent with their own families. There's a disquieting, nagging sense that we should *be with* each other more and great frustration over how to make that happen in our pressured lives.

Clearly, it is futile to wish for a "simpler" time, when Mother was home to handle the household and greet the children after school. For the majority of American parents with young children, that family configuration is not possible today. Happily, however, we are reevaluating the spurious concept of "quality time," a well-intentioned response to the reality of working mothers that only burdened already pressured parents with a compulsion to engineer "meaningful" get-togethers with their children. While we may, in fact, have fewer hours to spend together as a family than was true a generation or so ago, there are so many small ways to make loving, nurturing connections, if only we remember what children treasure. It is not so often the gifts or the elaborately planned outings. It's a hug, a quick trip to the Dairy Queen for an ice cream cone and a chat, a few minutes playing with the dog in the backyard. Children, even those oh-so-independent adolescents, love to do things with their families. Not to have more "things" but to do things together—this is what children want.

Small Gestures, Big Rewards

Many parents devote only weekend time to their children, and while it's certainly fine to have Saturday activities lined up, I encourage parents to think of ways to find more hours during the week to be with their children. Some parents are fortunate enough to be able to arrange their work schedules to allow for occasional afternoons off, time to spend with their children. One mother I talked to was entitled to a yearly four-week vacation from her job. She took two weeks for a family vacation; the remaining two weeks she arranged to take as a series of half days—twenty afternoons that she and her school-age daughter spent hanging out together, visiting a museum, going shopping, sitting in the park feeding the squirrels. Occasionally, mother and daughter arranged to pick up Dad when he got off work, and all three took in an early-evening movie together.

I like the idea of connecting with our children in some way during their school day, and children usually love it. This is their world, after all, and they relish having their parents see them in it. If a child is on a school athletic team, Dad or Mom might stop by to watch an afternoon practice, which can make a child feel just as pleased and proud as when his folks come to see the full-dress events. It's nice for a child to be able to introduce his dad or mom to the coach and his team members.

Visit a child during lunch hour at school. I always made a practice of doing this when my children were young, although it was a bit of a shocker at first—people wondered what problem had brought me to school during the day. I made it clear that nothing was wrong; I just felt it would be fun to have lunch with my son or daughter. And Eric and Pia came to look forward to it. Even their friends allowed that "It was nice of your dad to do that." Some schools might balk at the idea of parents visiting the lunchroom, but if the idea appeals to a parent, she might talk to the school PTA or administrators and try to establish such a policy about parent lunch visits. The practice need not interfere with school procedures or teaching schedules.

Make appointments with your children, planned "times out" together that they can look forward to, and make sure you keep them. Breaking a commitment to do something together is terribly hurtful to a child. She senses that she is not really terribly important in the parent's life, if a promise is so cavalierly broken. "We'll do it next week instead" is no comfort. I used to make dates with my children to go ice skating after school and I blocked off several hours during winter weeks when I didn't see patients or schedule meetings. I'd pick up the kids after school, we'd head for Rockefeller Center, and for an hour or so we'd relish our time together on the ice. A mother I counseled was having a rough patch with her teenage daughter who elected to spend all her after-school time with her friends. The mother made a shopping date with her daughter: "Next Thursday, after school, will you come shopping with me? I'd really love to have you help me pick out a new dress." The girl was charmed by the prospect of doing something with her mother and mentioned their planned shopping spree several times in the days leading up to it. Even recalcitrant teenagers usually respond to the promise of individual time with a mother or father and to a parent's expressed desire to be with them.

Spend time together by drawing a child into your activities. Rabid football-fan dads who cause their wives and children to feel widowed and orphaned during game time might try to share their particular passion by taking the time to explain strategies. So many fathers who work hard during the week feel entitled to enjoy the pleasure and relaxation of watching a game or playing a little Saturday golf. They are. But with a bit of renewed commitment and not much effort, those private pleasures can become shared activities and a true investment in the family.

Around a Kitchen Table: The Family Meal

Most of the people interviewed in a recent *New York Times/ CBS News* poll claimed that getting the family together for dinner was very important to them and that, in fact, on a typical week night, they did all eat together. But more than two-thirds also said the meal was over in thirty minutes or less, and close to half admitted to dining with the television in the background. So many of us, it seems, are squandering this most precious opportunity to spend time together—the family meal. Not only is it a time parents and children can join together to do the one thing each individually must—that is, eat—but it's the perfect forum in which to model manners and politeness, establish and practice nurturing family rituals, such as saying grace, dressing up a bit or eating by candlelight, and finding out what's going on in each other's lives. There's something about sharing food that facilitates conversation, provided there's no television set within thirty feet.

My own observations have been that many people eat on the run or in bits and pieces. Breakfast is frequently chaotic, a slap-dash affair as children down a quick glass of milk and some toast while they gather up school belongings, and parents grab a quick something on the run. I know many working couples who find it easier to feed the children dinner first, perhaps on a tray in front of the TV set, and then eat by themselves later. Preteens and adolescents in the habit of grazing at the refrigerator see no particular need for a "regular" meal.

It takes effort to reverse course in a family in which meals are a matter of every man for himself or a necessity to be got through as quickly as possible. Certainly with two-career parents and heavily scheduled children, connecting at dinnertime takes both planning and resolve. Eliminate television. If a family member desperately must catch a particular program that airs during dinner, perhaps you can tape it. If your teenager says, thanks, but he's not really hungry and his friends are waiting, tell him "Then tomorrow night I want all of us to eat together. If you're not going to be there, we'll miss you and we won't feel like we're a family. So plan to join us." Relax rules about green vegetables and chicken-before-dessert. Be ready to ignore food complaints and routine messiness.

A meal is never just the eating of food. To me, cooking has always been a family activity, and I taught my children to cook—in a simple way, of course—at an early age. Preparing a meal together can be a marvelous time for the family to pitch in and have real fun in the kitchen. Recipes can be selected, lettuce can be washed, the table needs to be set and cleared, dishes washed. Even the littlest children can have something to do and feel a part of this vital family function.

The best dinner table talk happens spontaneously, with no one on the carpet for a grilling. Saying to a child, "So, what did you do in school today?" almost inevitably leads to the reply, "I don't know . . . nothing special." Children hate feeling they're being interrogated. Just get a conversation going. It may have to do with what happened in your office that day, a project you're involved in, a coworker who's giving you a hard time. Children like it when parents share their woes. When my children were young and living at home, I would sometimes complain at the dinner table about an injustice perpetrated on me, and I'd hear a lot of advice. If nothing else, it let my children know that I had problems, too. And just as often as not, my children opened up and began to talk about their own concerns. Children need to realize that being a grown-up doesn't mean being free of frustrations and that those frustrations are not all that unlike those they may be having with their friends, schools and teachers. Almost coincidentally, or as an aside to a conversation in progress, children will reveal things you might never have realized about their interests, concerns and feelings. Share the time over a meal, focus on each other, eliminate distractions and the good stuff will happen.

When you invite your own friends for an evening, invite your children and their friends to share the dinner. Spread the children out, interspersed with grown-ups, so that everyone engages in the same talk and the children are not grouped at one end of the table, where they giggle their way through the meal. Whether the conversation is about politics or personalities or food or a little good gossipy news, the children benefit and learn. They may be actively engaged in the talk or sitting mute but obviously attentive—just to hear adults swapping information and ideas and life experiences in an atmosphere of mutual respect is a lesson in values.

Recently, I consulted with a family that included four children. Three of the four complained that their eleven-year-old sister, Nora, was a terrible nuisance. When I asked for an example, one sibling said, "When we go to McDonald's, Nora wants different stuff on her hamburger instead of the regular stuff that's already made. So we all have to wait longer." Perhaps Nora's siblings had other gripes against Nora and "different stuff on the hamburger" was only the tip of the iceberg, so to speak, but their annoyance over this issue was a vivid demonstration to me of how as a society we have become inculcated by the fast-food mentality and the notion that eating is something to be got over with as quickly as possible. We should work to bring back the tradition of the family meal and recognize that cooking is an art form, a way of doing special caring things for the family that please the basic senses of taste and smell. Some of the best home time can happen around a gracious table, with the family gathered, with satisfying food consumed at a leisurely pace, with everyone talking and sharing.

If it were possible to mandate that every family in America have breakfast and dinner together every day, I'm convinced we would see a tremendous change in the quality and process of communication, mutual understanding and reinforcement of family values.

Special Times: Vacations and Holidays

Those "time-out" times of the year when we abandon for a while our normal school and work routines are rich with opportunities for special ways of sharing ourselves, establishing family rituals and traditions, doing the things that make for happy memories. Vacation for my family over the years has been to go to the north woods of Maine, where we enjoy a completely different set of routines, a departure from our day-to-day life in New York. There's no television. We're close to Nature, getting around in boats, repairing things ourselves. We split our own wood and generate our own electricity. We don't get dressed up. *The New York Times* is a day old when it arrives by mail, which turns out to be perfectly okay. Although I'm something of a news junkie, I've learned I can survive very nicely without the morning talk shows and the eleven o'clock news. What comes through on the radio up in the wilderness of Maine is reports of fishing conditions and logging contests; once an hour, there is thirty seconds of international reporting, just enough to let us know the world is still there. At night, we play games or read, have cookouts or take the boats out for stargazing; most nights friends join us. We create our own social world, one we all share.

Holidays can be a time of wild extremes—excited anticipation, gaiety and partying, overstimulation and disappointment, and even depression. A time when increased interactions among relatives and friends and shared rituals can give both a nourishing sense of continuity and connection to the past and the opportunity for frayed nerves and sputtering irritations. Many people anticipate the family holiday get-togethers with some dread—Cousin Mary plays one-upmanship games concerning her children's accomplishments; Uncle Jack has too much to drink and turns belligerent. And yet, for most of us, joining with family members, warts and all, is powerfully satisfying and necessary. After all, these are the people who in large measure define us, where we have come from and what shared genes and history have shaped us. And what a fertile field in which to expand the parameters of family and to instill in our children a more sensitive awareness of the power of respect, responsibility and caring.

My immediate family always gathers at Thanksgiving, as many as can manage, and we have great good times together. But we also always look among our friends, and even people we may not yet know very well, to see who may be alone for the holiday and include them in our family celebration. Last Thanksgiving, we invited one of the doctors who had treated me in the hospital during my illness. Dr. Bob Helm, a young intern, had shown great compassion toward me in small ways, and I felt that he had become part of my life in some way. It seemed fitting and natural to make him and his fiancée part of our Thanksgiving family. One of the pleasures of adulthood is being able to structure holiday gatherings the way *you* want, to reshape and fine-tune the details and to get maximum gratification from the festivities. To leave one's own stamp on memories in the making.

So many parents I talk to despair about their children's "greediness" during Christmas and Hanukkah. They worry that the demands for toys and gifts are a sign of selfishness, or worse, the dreaded spoiled child. But a child's wanting lots of things really does not indicate greediness; it is a reaction to the excitement, the indulgence and the departure from the constraints adults attempt to exercise throughout the rest of the year. Festive, fancy foods are consumed in more than normal quantities, parties are going on, friends visit—and the scope of our wishes and desires is also fattened and extended. Since Christmas and Hanukkah are so focused on them, children are even more intensely stimulated; tantalizing, ever-present advertisements for toys, along with grown-ups demanding to know what they want for Christmas, further heighten the excitement. Certainly, there's a letdown after a child has opened all her presents, but it is more because the gift giving has come to an end than because, greedily, she regrets that she did not get all she wanted. The disappointment is really about reentry into the normal world of all the un-Christmassy days ahead.

It's awfully difficult for parents to stem the tide of holiday commercialism, but parents can set a "noncommercial" example for their children and demonstrate their deeper beliefs. If a mother sees the holidays as a time for celebrating, sharing and exchanging tokens of real affection, she can do it in a way that doesn't require endless sums of money. If she bakes a batch of special cookies that Aunt Joan likes, or sends a gift subscription to a cousin's favorite magazine, or frames a child's school drawing that Grandma admired, her children will come to appreciate that the thoughtfulness behind a gift conveys the most meaning to the person receiving it.

Even very young children can learn a lesson in sharing. Have your children go through their playthings and pick out not only those they might have outgrown, but some they still like very much and feel another child might also enjoy. Suggest they clean up these items and donate them to a community organization that distributes toys to children who are not likely to get gifts otherwise. Don't simply gather the toys yourself, but have your youngsters participate fully in the process—and have *them* make the presentation to the charitable organization so they can gain the recognition that usually comes with that kind of sharing and generosity. After all, this might be a good way for your children to learn for themselves who Santa Claus really is. By being little Santas themselves, they may come to understand that *real people* are the ones who give the presents.

Most children adore the traditions associated with the religious holidays and get even more caught up in them than adults do. Accounts of the "old days" can have a vivid and intense meaning for children. Reading stories, telling them about your own childhood, and passing on the recollections of grandparents and other relatives serve to maintain the continuity of spirit and meaning of your own background and beliefs. If the holiday season is a meaningful experience for parents, if it is one that involves understanding, love and the expression of thoughtfulness for others, children of any age will feel it.

Hugs and Kisses, Routines and Rituals

I once counseled a father who was terribly worried because he was unable to spend much time with his children. He was at a point in his job life that required him to work long hours and to travel several days a month. He sensed some missing intimacy, even though he was a full participant with his wife in all decisions concerning his son and daughter and went to great effort to be on hand for parent-teacher conferences and school plays and demonstrated his concern and caring by spending his available home hours helping with homework and taking his children places. He felt the solution lay in more time together, and that he couldn't manage. I asked him how frequently he hugged and kissed his children. He wasn't a big hugger and kisser, it turned out, and his ten-year-old son in particular, he felt, "wouldn't put up with that." I disagreed and suggested he focus less, for a while, on their time apart, which he couldn't change, and more on their time together. I suggested short, sweet, physical displays of love for his children that he might foster.

Not all people feel comfortable being demonstrative about their feelings, even with those closest to them. That reticence can be a family or cultural trait, or a matter of personality. But I encourage parents to show their love by hugging their children—no matter how old they are. Hug them, hold them, give them kisses. We know that infants thrive in relation to how often they are held. Babies who are not picked up, even if they are fed and kept warm and dry, wither and withdraw. All humans need physical affection, and such displays are one vital way that families communicate love. And something good happens when two people hug. A popular program of marriage therapy includes "The Sixty-Second Hug." As part of their efforts to overcome feelings of estrangement or anger and to open up communication, couples are urged to spend one minute a day in a simple, nonsexual, uninterrupted hug. Obviously, troubled marriages aren't instantly healed, but even battling couples can come away smiling.

My father and I always hugged and kissed. I remember when I went off to the war, my father took me to the train station. He took his watch off, the only thing he had to give, and put it on my wrist. Then we put our arms around each other and hugged. I remember looking around at the other departing soldiers, many with their families; their fathers kept their distance, gave their sons a hearty handshake or a slap on the back, saying, "Well, good luck, son." I remember, too, some of them looking at my father and me as if there were something strange about us. And to us, showing our love by holding each other was as normal as talking.

My brothers and I hug and kiss each other and show affection, and I've always been equally demonstrative with my son. Now he leans down and kisses me on top of my bald head, and considers that both important and absolutely normal. Touching and being openly affectionate is not histrionic; it demonstrates real love. It's part of being a family.

Children adore the small, loving rituals of daily home time that create a feeling of safe haven and reassuring continuity. A single mother and her daughter *always* stay up late on Friday night to curl up on the couch with popcorn and a rented movie. Dad *always* takes his sons along on Saturday morning when he does neighborhood chores, and they *always* finish up at McDonald's for burgers and shakes. Mornings include five minutes of Mom and the kids doing silly stretching exercises to the music on the radio. Nighttimes include ten minutes of Dad coming into the bedroom to read or chat or say prayers.

Bedtime rituals are especially reassuring to children and a good way to demonstrate respect for a child's feelings. Unfortunately, bedtime in many families means "war" time, with struggles, on the one hand, to stay up later, and, on the other, to "get in bed and stay there." We often put children to bed before they are ready and insist on more sleep than they really need. Withdrawing from the waking world to go off into the world of sleep is a transition that's sometimes difficult, even scary. It helps to have fatigue on your side.

If you know your child is just about ready to be coaxed into sleep, that's a good time to sit down with her, quietly, talk a little, read to her. Almost all children of every age, even young adolescents, love to be read to at night, which can be difficult for hardworking parents who are themselves fatigued. At a certain age, my own children loved hearing *Winnie-the-Pooh.* I recall many times that I fell asleep before my child did. Just creating that peaceful atmosphere was enough to lull me.

The bedtime reading ritual, like all the other small, habitual demonstrations of love and support, enriches our moments together and creates a shared history, one that's comforting to all family members.

Bad Moods and Just Plain Fights

The happiest families sometimes have disagreements. Loving couples from time to time blow up at each other. Moms and dads with constitutionally happy, sunny dispositions have off days, bad-mood attacks, or personal idiosyncrasies that when triggered lead to out-of-character fumes and spats. All these minor downsides to human nature and day-to-day living are inevitably part of the richness of family life. And children need to know that.

My son and daughter understood very well as they were growing up that their dad was occasionally in a bad mood, under stress, even downright crabby. I was never reluctant to say, "I'm sorry, I'm really not in a very good mood. I had a bad day at work. I need you not to bug me tonight." My children respected that, and consequently, I think, felt free to acknowledge their own bad moods. Pia has said more than once, "Sorry, Dad, but I'm in a bad mood today. And you know what it's like to be in a bad mood." And I've said, "Yes, I certainly do."

Parents, of course, can't be perfect—and how uncomfortable for our children it would be if we were. Your children are better off knowing your weaknesses—and knowing that *you* know them and can be a bit rueful and jocular about them. To indicate to a child that "This is something about me that I know is a little unpredictable, unpleasant or off the wall; it's something that you just have to learn to tolerate because it's a minor offense or won't last long" is to foster the child's respect. I am irrationally annoyed when people spill things on the floor, and my children have felt those small blasts of annoyance many times over the years. They tolerate with good humor what they clearly see as a silly but harmless quirk. My son once said, "Dad, I'm tempted to take something and just pour it all over the floor in front of you, you're so fussy about it." To which I replied, "Well, try it sometime if it will make you happy." So far, he hasn't.

So many parents I have counseled worry about arguing in front of their children. They think the children will be upset and fearful and so it's better to keep these disagreements private. But really, an argument is a normal part of life, a difference of opinion between two people and an attempt to resolve that difference. For this reason, having a child witness an argument can actually be a most beneficial and rewarding experience, providing her parents explain that "We were sort of angry and shouting at each other, but just because Mommy and Daddy are having an argument doesn't mean we don't love each other. People who love each other have differences of opinion because they're different people. I know you love both of us very much, but you love us differently because we're different people. Different people sometimes disagree with each other and get mad, even though they love each other."

If your child can watch you argue and see that you are still affectionate toward each other, though not necessarily at the moment, she's learning a little lesson in how to cope with her own feelings of anger. If she never sees you angry, she may begin to feel guilty about her own feelings of anger and resentment when they occur, as they surely will. She may feel that something is wrong with her because she is having feelings that are unacceptable.

Be open about your disagreements, but always argue with dignity and show respect for your partner. Arguments that include abusive statements, objects being thrown or destroyed, or any kind of physical abuse are terribly upsetting to a child, who can hardly be expected to come to terms with his own anger now that he's witnessed his parents lose control of theirs. If your child sees you out of control in these ways, his ensuing anxiety is based on his completely appropriate understanding that he cannot rely on people with such tendencies to protect him. Fears, nightmares and panic reactions often haunt a child following an episode where parents carry an argument to the point of physical abuse or degrading remarks aimed at each other.

Parents who think it's wrong to express anger or annoyance toward each other in front of their children often conduct their arguments behind closed doors, believing their children will remain unaware of any unpleasantness. But while youngsters may be protected from knowing the details of the argument, they are always fully aware of the emotions. Mom and Dad's conversations with each other are tense, cold and sharp, and this alone tells children that something is wrong. A child may entertain fantasies about what's going on that are far worse than the reality. If parents persist in hiding normal disagreements, a child learns to live in a dual world: one where he experiences his true emotions, and another where he feigns certain emotions in an effort to please his parents. Far better that he hear Mom and Dad be angry with each other now and then.

Children are wise and instinctual creatures, capable of understanding the subtext without the words. An open, healthy, clear-the-air argument between parents shows the child that all kinds of feelings, even upsetting ones, are quite normal and gives some real-life at-home experience in how problems get solved.

A Father's Role

Around 1970, I was asked to write a cover story on fatherhood for a national magazine. I said, "I'll do it on the condition that you put a father holding a baby on the cover." They did, and that cover was rather startling to see. Men didn't hold babies very often twenty years ago, at least not on magazine covers. Today, of course, fathers carrying babies in slings and pushing strollers are common sights.

I have been a fierce advocate of father involvement in children's lives since the beginning of my professional career in the early 1950s and have always felt fathers should be encouraged to participate in every aspect of a child's development, from birth to adulthood. I pioneered the movement to involve fathers in labor and delivery at a time when it was totally unfashionable and, in some hospitals, virtually outlawed. During the birth of my son, I remember, I was forbidden to enter the delivery room and had to fight my way into the labor room and insist on rooming-in for the baby and his mother. Today, allowing fathers in the labor and delivery rooms is standard procedure, due partly to the persuasive efforts and work of lay organizations and partly to the economic reality that hospitals that allowed these family privileges were better patronized. There is still not a great deal of institutional encouragement for father participation.

Childbirth must be seen as a family experience, not as a medical procedure. Fathers should be present not only in the labor and delivery rooms, but in the diapering and feeding classes in the hospital or birthing center. These skills should not be left for the mothers to teach the fathers. In the 1960s, I instituted a requirement that both parents be present for my parenting classes. I learned in later follow-ups with fathers who had been involved in the delivery of their children that almost all experienced great happiness and pleasure in holding, kissing, feeding and even diapering their babies, emotions not ordinarily admitted to by men of that era. I think siblings should be encouraged to visit their mother and see the new baby as soon as he or she is born. Such visits can be wonderfully effective in relieving the feelings of isolation older children have at this time and minimizing potential sibling rivalry.

A medical establishment should convey in no uncertain terms that fathers are expected to care for their children. Some years ago, at a United Nations meeting on childbirth in America, I advocated the idea that the birth of a child be celebrated by the hospital. I suggested the hospital might offer to celebrate the new family with a candlelight dinner for Mother and Father, perhaps including a bottle of wine and flowers. I've talked to more than one father who has felt somewhat left out of the proceedings and a bit resentful because a meal was brought to his wife after the delivery, but he was not included. A family meal is now standard procedure in some hospitals, but not many.

It's often hard for a willing father to feel like a full participant in his child's life. Hospitals, schools and workplaces seem almost to conspire against his presence, and the very term "fathering," with its connotation of merely the act of procreation, has a far more limited implication than "mothering." I like the concept of the word "parenting," which can incorporate the loving behavior of a mother in the repertoire of a father's responsibilities, commitments and activities. There is overwhelming clinical and other research evidence showing that fathers who are affectionate, demonstrative, engaged in raising children from birth, and significant in a child's life because they set limits and are consistent, help that child develop high self-esteem and form solid relationships all through life.

5

Building a Structure of Values

"My son always told me, 'Dad, I'm your son, but you treat me like an independent person. You don't rule over me. I'm my own person and you respect me that way.' And I do."

THERE IS ABSOLUTELY no way a parent can get from one day to another without experiencing problems. There's no such thing as having family responsibilities and raising children without encountering paradoxical situations all along the way. And most parents from time to time feel that only *they* are overwhelmed and only *their* youngster is acting up or talking back, running wild or getting fresh, being a public nuisance or a downright embarrassment.

In our better moments, we realize that that isn't the case and that most of our parent peers are bumbling and struggling in a similar manner on the road to producing the next generation of adults. But in the day-to-day business of parenting, we can sometimes feel awfully alone and uncertain. Children move through higher and higher levels of independence. At each step, the child separates a little more from her parents, becomes a little more her own person. Each step involves a push-pull on both sides that's both absolutely appropriate and healthy, and, at the same time, a bit scary for child and parent alike.

All parents would agree, I think, that in the broadest terms their goal is to raise a responsible child. The popular movie *Home Alone* showed a little boy who was accidentally left behind by his parents when they went off to Paris at Christmas. Among other reasons, I believe the movie had such appeal because the boy was able to master his separation from his parents. He was given, accidentally, a chance to behave responsibly; he did, and he received a lot of recognition because of it. Moviegoers could appreciate the boy's accomplishment—it's one that both parents and children heartily desire.

Living up to one's responsibilities was one of the key eight family values Americans reported in the Mellman & Lazarus study and, in fact, the quality respondents felt was most critical to the way they lived their personal lives. Many participants talked of the basic responsibilities of going to work, earning money and supporting a family, and of feelings of generalized responsibility to coworkers and society at large. But many also clearly held deep convictions about the need for all family members to be responsible for and to each other, children as well as grown-ups. Said one, "As part of a family, you've got an obligation to every member of that family."

In my years of counseling families, I've listened to hundreds of parents struggle with the issues involved in raising children to be responsible for their actions, issues that so often revolve around questions of discipline. Should we be logical, and reason with our children? Should we punish a child for misbehaving by spanking or taking away privileges? What are the best ways to make children "behave"?

There really are no tricks or shortcuts. Parents need to recognize that at each age and stage a child needs limits.

The "No" Word

I counseled a very charming, sweet couple, earnestly well-intentioned parents who were determined not to saddle their child with middle-class values or to frustrate him unnecessarily. They told me, "We've never said no to our son on anything." But they had come to me because their boy was anxious, jittery, and showed no self-control.

I asked them, "Why don't you ever say no?"

"Well," the mother said, "it's so *negative.*"

I said, "I know. It's *meant* to be negative. The purpose of 'No' is to put limits on behavior. How can the word 'Yes' and the concept of freedom have any meaning unless there is 'No' and the concept of restrictions?"

So many parents I talk to have an inordinately difficult time with this most direct and immediate method of setting limits. Often their reluctance to be "negative" stems from their own childhood disappointments and resentment of what they remember as punitive or restricting parents. A friend told me, "My mother was so frustrating because she never listened to what I wanted or was saying. I got to hate her. I don't want my child to hate me, so I really try to respect everything he wants."

This child, now seven, wrings his hands a lot and acts terribly nervous. His need for immediate gratification is enormous. He actually says, "I want it, and I want it *now.*" He has trouble getting along with other children, doesn't smile and usually doesn't say hello or goodbye. He masters challenges quite well and is extremely bright. He's just not a particularly pleasant child to be with.

One morning, at our house, he helped my daughter make a cake for the meal we were all to share that evening. The boy helped out by sifting a little bit of the flour and cracking the eggs. That afternoon, his mother asked me if he could have a piece of the cake now.

I said, "Can he wait until dinnertime and have it when everybody else does?"

My friend explained, "Well, he sort of wants it now."

"You know," I said, "if he has to have it now I guess he can, but why exactly can't he wait until later?"

"I want him to feel that since he did the flour sifting, there's a reward for him," she said. "He's helped mix the ingredients and seen them baked into the cake, and now he wants the results of what he's done."

I continued to make my point, to a still-resistant audience. "Quite frankly," I told her, "I think John shouldn't be allowed to have the cake now. And you can explain that to him, because he's old enough to understand. There are several reasons why he should wait to eat the cake when everybody else does. Tell him that if you cut into the cake now, it will have to be all wrapped up to keep it from getting stale, and that we planned to show off a beautiful chocolate cake at the dinner table before we cut it into pieces."

After much deliberation, my friend decided not to let her son have a piece of cake. I then used that as a springboard for a little talk about how she might think about preparing John for the real world.

I can understand my friend's motivation. She wants her boy to be able to do what he wants; she doesn't want to thwart his creativity or his need for reward; and she wants him to love her—all perfectly appropriate parental desires, but carried to an extreme that causes her to lose sight of her parental responsibilities. This degree of tolerance is neither supportive nor respectful. It cripples the child, who goes through critical stages of development without learning to deal with frustration. He's in real danger of failing to learn his earliest lessons in coping with stress or difficulties, lessons that are awfully hard to teach at a later stage. It's a bit like a puppy whose owners have not made the effort to housebreak it within the first six months; the puppy is past the point where he can learn that necessary behavior.

The ideal of freedom doesn't permit us to exercise our personal rights whenever, however or wherever we wish; that's a lesson children should assimilate step by step all the way to adulthood. Children must learn that creative, exploratory or personally enjoyable behaviors have to be balanced with concern for others' rights and feelings—with manners, in other words. We all have had the misfortune, in restaurants or other public places, of seeing children who run, yell or generally disrupt the rest of us, children whose parents probably have been led to believe that inhibiting a child's free expression is unhealthy.

While I very much like the idea of taking children of all ages to restaurants, I also believe in setting limits beforehand. Ask your child, "Would you like to come? Yes? Then I'll expect you to sit and speak in a quiet manner and not throw food or do anything that disturbs people, because that's not fair." If the child does misbehave, on the next going-out evening her parents must say, "We're not taking you with us because the last time we went to a restaurant you didn't follow the rules we agreed on. That's why you're going to stay home with the baby-sitter tonight. Would you like to try again the next time we go out?"

Even very young children, from the time they are able to move around in their environment, are capable of appreciating "No" rules and regulations, as long as they are set at a level the child can comprehend. Thus, while it is quite possible to teach an eight- or nine-month-old that it's all right to tear newspapers but not magazines, it is not possible to teach her that she can tear yesterday's paper but not today's. Since she has not learned to read words or recognize dates, the distinction between yesterday's paper and today's is beyond her.

If you are surprised that a child under a year old can be taught not to tear magazines, while she's allowed to destroy newspapers, let me explain how it's done. Allow your child to approach a coffee table piled with magazines and newspapers. She'll begin playing with them and will glance at you to discover your reaction as she explores the piles. As she begins to tear a magazine, take it away, say "No" very firmly, and be emphatic in expressing your annoyance so that your displeasure is clearly understood. Simply murmuring "No" while smiling at a young child will probably not register. Although you must make your dissatisfaction absolutely clear, do not act so displeased that your child stops understanding your displeasure and becomes afraid. Now give the magazine back to her. More than likely, if she has not been frightened into stopping her efforts to learn, she'll make another attempt to tear the magazine, and you should again react in exactly the same way. She's beginning to understand the consistent pattern in your behavior.

She will probably go on to repeat her action several times in varying ways to establish clearly that you are indeed reacting to what she is doing and that you really mean what you say. Actually, she thinks all this is sort of a game. To make your point absolutely clear, somewhere along the line you can pick up a newspaper, tear it, and then show your child that she may tear the paper. After she's done so, she may again try to tear the magazine, and again you'll give her your firm "No." Your child may have to repeat the experiment involving the newspaper and magazine a number of times before she learns exactly what the rules and regulations that govern this particular behavior are. If you're going to teach her not to rip up magazines, you'll have to allow a lot of time and be very patient.

Saying no by setting clear limits on what is acceptable and what is not, being ready to do it again and again, treating the child with respect and understanding—these are the critical ingredients parents need to bring up children who are both responsible and delightful.

Just Plain Good Manners

It's a pleasure for me to watch my children in action. When they're with me, they're quite outspoken, often blunt, and not necessarily diplomatic in their expressions. When an argument has become heated, when an amiable disagreement has escalated, they invariably acknowledge that perhaps they've gone too far and say, "Sorry, Dad, I didn't mean to shout or say it like that." My response is, "It's all right. I'm glad you express yourself." They are confident enough in our love to disagree, argue and even tell me exactly what they think is wrong with me. That's what families are all about.

But when my son and daughter meet strangers or interact with people outside the family, they're always polite, always respectful. I feel that my efforts in raising their consciousness about respecting people, and in modeling that respect myself, were a success. Good manners are really just a way of showing respect. And even children as young as toddlers can begin to learn what that's all about—in the home, where respect always begins.

When children are around eighteen months of age, they imitate a great deal of their parents' social behavior. The youngster picks up the bad and the good habits he sees demonstrated by his all-powerful parents. If his parents habitually greet each other in the morning with a smile and a kiss and a cheery "Good morning, how did you sleep last night?" the child learns that this is the way people act with each other. If parents are careless in their mealtime habits, reaching and grabbing, forgetting the "Please" and "Thank you," he will probably do the same.

I remember when my mother died and our relatives came back to our house after the funeral. My son, Eric, about two and a half, was the focus of much attention from these virtual strangers, all eager to hug and kiss him. As one relative was reaching out to grab him in a big hug, Eric pointed to a passing aunt and said, "Would you like to kiss her instead?" Clearly, he thought he saw a way to evade the kisses and be polite at the same time.

By respecting the small child's desire to imitate you, you can encourage good manners with a smile, a positive attitude, recognition of her efforts and a consistent display of your own politeness around the dinner table and in all the other small daily interactions of family life. Small children make mistakes. They need to be reminded, usually many times, of what is expected. Making a game out of things can sometimes be a wonderful way to get across important information. In the mind of a young child, there's a bit of magic in finding that when you pass the salt to a grown-up, he or she automatically says "Thank you" with a smile. A little exaggeration now and then gets the point across very well. If you are overly emphatic in your politeness, the child is sure to notice and believe that what you are doing must be very important indeed. If on occasion your own manners flag, your child will probably be amused if you say, "Oops! You'd better take the salt back from me—I forgot to say thank you!"

It is possible to "train" a child in mannerly behavior by hammering and nagging in a punitive way, but how much better if those same goals are accomplished in an atmosphere of pleasantness. Then, those values of respect and politeness become part of the child's normal behavior because she *wants* to act that way, not because she's afraid of punishment; that's a feeling that will serve her well as she grows and her relationships with the world at large become more complex, her awareness of other people's feelings and differences becomes deeper.

A four- or five-year-old walking down the street sees a badly crippled person with canes coming toward him and asks his mother, "Why does that person walk funny?" Or says to a neighbor, "How did you get so fat?" Punishing the child for being rude will only confuse him if, like most thoroughly modern American children, he has been taught to be honest and to ask questions about things that puzzle him. The parent in that momentary but acutely embarrassing situation can say quietly to her son, "I can understand that you want an answer to your question, but sometimes asking such things can hurt people's feelings. What we have to do sometimes is whisper between ourselves or talk about these things when that person is not around."

Teaching a child to be polite is really a matter of helping him learn all the small social rules that make all our daily interactions with the world run more smoothly. Adults know that when a casual friend asks "How are you? How are you feeling?" what is called for is not a litany of one's current aches and pains and misfortunes, but a simple, "Fine, thank you. How are you?" Or that Aunt Greta's gift of a particularly atrocious candelabra can be acknowledged as an act of kindness if not good taste. A child learns these lessons in diplomacy over time as a parent models appropriate behavior and as she urges him gently toward attitudes of greater empathy and understanding. If your child receives a sweater he thinks is ugly and itchy, you can say, "You must remember that your cousin gave you a gift, which means it's something you receive without expecting it. She probably gave a lot of thought to choosing this and went out of her way to buy it for you. I know you don't like it much, but you can thank her for how nice she was to think of you." Such a comment acknowledges the child's feelings but shows him that he doesn't really have to share them with the gift giver. He can accept the unfortunate gift in a way that's both honest and tactful.

Ideally, children come to appreciate that polite behavior and awareness of others' feelings makes them feel good. I like the idea of saying to a child now and then, "You know that special warm feeling you get when people say nice things about you, or thank you for something you've done? It makes you feel good, doesn't it?" Reinforce the idea that your child's behavior has ramifications, and that one of those ramifications is that he'll feel good about himself.

What's Wrong with Spanking?

Whenever I write a magazine article, or respond on television to a question about corporal punishment, I receive a flood of "Spare the rod and spoil the child" mail protesting my position.

So many people still believe that hitting children is an appropriate and effective way to control them, even, most shockingly, young babies. On a radio call-in program recently, a man phoned with some questions about making his children "mind," and acknowledged that he sometimes hit his nine-month-old son. I said, "With all due respect, I must tell you, you don't hit babies. It's cruel." His response: "I'm not going to let that baby dominate my life."

We are living in a culture that too often brutalizes its children. Hitting an infant is an extreme example, but the justification expressed by that father demonstrates an all-too-common notion: that children need to be "controlled" by being shown that parents have the upper hand. Proponents of spanking claim that it "straightens children out," "gets them to do what you want." While it may in fact get children to "behave" or "perform" at that particular moment, in the long run it can have devastating effects. I'm convinced that almost *every* child or young person who becomes destructive and hostile toward figures or institutions of authority is retaliating in some way against a parent or parent surrogate who brutalized the child in some physical way in the past.

Punishing a child by spanking or slapping her does not convince her that something she's done is wrong. All it does is persuade the child that her parent is angry, out of control, unreasonable, someone to be feared. She can actually feel self-righteous rather than repentant and come away with the lesson that "Next time I'd better be careful and not get caught." She has learned, in other words, to control herself to avoid punishment, rather than to deal with the concept that her behavior is not acceptable. What we want children to develop is a conscience—a humane and compassionate concept of right and wrong—rather than a superficial shrewdness about staying out of trouble.

I have counseled a substantial number of adults who remember a childhood spanking as a turning point in their relationship with a parent. While the spanking appeared to do its punitive job, it also created tremendous resentment and fear in the child. Those feelings interfered with the communication between parent and child for the rest of their lives. The spanking transformed the relationship in an irreversible way. As one young man told me, "I could never, ever talk to my father in the same way again after that happened."

Think of what a parent is teaching when she spanks or hits her child, whatever the circumstances. She is conveying the message that it's all right for human beings to use physical force to make smaller or weaker human beings do things they don't want to do. I believe it is not exaggerating to say that a parent who spanks is a parent who is condoning violence and exploitation. And usually the child is stunned and humiliated. Just the idea that "Somebody's hitting me . . . my mom is slapping me" is shocking.

Of course children need to learn how to behave. They need to learn when they do things that hurt or annoy or anger others. They need to experience the consequences of their behavior, and if that behavior involves destructive actions, to be in some way responsible for restitution. They need to pay a price.

The most powerful price can be a loving parent's displeasure. While I'm absolutely opposed to spanking and any kind of physical violence toward a child, I'm not against the vigorous expression of annoyance. In fact, showing your feelings, from disappointment to steaming mad, is absolutely essential to let children know you don't like what they've done.

When my children were younger, I often heard myself saying, "Now don't do that anymore!" Like most children, they just as often continued the forbidden behavior, and, like most parents, I would feel increasingly annoyed. I rarely punished Eric or Pia by taking away treats or pleasures. To deny the ice cream or the television viewing time simply increases the perceived value of those things. Sending a child to bed early for misbehavior makes going to bed punitive, and the bedtime ritual should be a pleasant, comforting activity. "Grounding" or sending a child to his room for the day doesn't work very well.

Invariably, my most effective tactic was a clear, honest expression of my feelings. I would say, "Look, I'm very annoyed with you because you disobeyed me. I don't really want to talk to you for a while. I don't feel like reading to you, I'm not going to play with you. I'll get over it, but I just want you to know that you've really, really upset me."

This bothered my children enormously. Guilt was writ large on their faces. After a short while had passed, my daughter would stroll over and say, "Are you over it yet, Dad?" I'd say, "Not quite." She'd say, "Okay," and maintain a low profile for another short stretch of time. Soon I'd say, "Okay, I'm over it now." And both sides were ready for a brief discussion of the behavior and back to business as usual.

When a child feels "Gosh, I hurt my dad; I hate to see him feeling bad because of what I did," she will be motivated to try to avoid a repeat performance. Guilt and remorse can lead to a sense of responsibility that spanking will never engender. You can get a child to "behave" simply by getting him to listen to how you feel and then thinking, in a respectful way, about what you're trying to convey.

At the end of a lecture during which I addressed the issue of spanking, a man came up to me and said, "When I was a kid and I did something wrong, my father spanked me, and it was over with. I felt great. If he'd done what you're suggesting, I would have felt like hell for a long time." I said, "That's why he should have done it, because then you would have incorporated into your value system what's acceptable and what's not. And you can take that with you wherever you go. But your father can't be there to spank you every time you do wrong." Spanking, in a very real sense, lets a child off the hook. Someone else is in charge of regulating his behavior.

Brothers and Sisters

The most understandable reaction in a parent eager to demonstrate that she loves all of her children equally is to say "I love you all exactly the same." Understandable, but a big mistake. The stage is set for the child to test, again and again, the absolute equality of his mother's attentions. Mother's "equal love" is on trial a hundred times a day. The child thinks, "I'll prove that you don't love us the same because you don't treat us the same," and then will, for example, count the number of chips in his chocolate chip cookie and the number in his sister's cookie to see who got more.

Well-meaning, loving efforts to minimize sibling rivalry in this absolutely-the-same way usually backfire. One father always asks friends to give the same gift to each of his two daughters at Christmas. He is extremely sensitive that his children may discern differences in the presents they receive, the time people spend with each, and their parents' expressions of affection. In fact, his children are more than normally aware of any differences, largely because their father goes to such extremes to avoid them. In such a situation, I would, if anything, encourage friends to give each child a different gift. If one sister likes the other's present more, I would point out that that's the way things are sometimes. Life has its frustrations; sometimes we all just have to accept disappointment, an excellent lesson in the realities of life with siblings.

No two people are alike, of course, and neither are children. Far better for a parent to recognize each child's individuality from the start and treat him accordingly. A mother or father can emphasize in various ways, and in so many words, "Everybody is different. We love each of you because you're unique, you're special and you're you." They can even say, "We love you all in different ways because you're different people. It's the way you feel about us. I know you love Daddy and Mommy very much, but you love us in different ways because we're different people."

Sibling rivalry is really not much different from the struggle all young children undergo to achieve recognition and attention from the adults caring for them. When a young child has his parents all to himself, life is fine. When the announcement is made that a new little brother or sister will be joining the family, he's not so sure at all that he likes the idea. From the young child's point of view, there's an awful lot of fuss and bother for a tiny baby that no one even knows yet! And he's also wondering: Why do you need a new baby, anyway? Why am I not good enough for you?" He may feel terribly threatened, fearful of losing what he holds most dear and downright resentful. At the same time, he probably shares some of the family's general enthusiasm and pleasant anticipation. Part of him wants to help in the preparations for the new baby, but part of him is thinking, "I want to be that baby everyone is getting so excited about."

Such perfectly normal feelings are intensified when the children are close in age. I believe strongly that children should be spaced at least three years apart, if possible, so that each child goes through her early stages of development as the focus of the parent's attention. Two-year-olds are demanding little people who still need tremendous amounts of parents' time and one-on-one attention. A somewhat older child, having conquered several of the critical challenges of the early years, such as weaning and toilet training, is less inclined to feel that this newcomer has "stolen" her time.

Even so, having a new baby come home from the hospital is a momentous occasion in a youngster's life—in some ways, an irreversible tragedy. Everyone is talking about this new individual, a total stranger who requires all kinds of delicate handling and who is admired by all. People discuss the new baby, who he resembles, how healthy he is, and just about everyone asks the baby's older sibling, "Aren't you happy that you have a new baby brother?" He's not so sure.

The best way for a parent to help an older child cope with this new development is to tell him openly very early on everything that will happen, both pleasant and unpleasant. In preparing my son, Eric, who was then five, for the birth of his sister, I emphasized the many negative aspects. I warned him that we wouldn't have as much time to spend with him alone, that we would no longer have the peace and quiet we were used to, that there would be a lot of fussing and crying in the middle of the night and in the midst of conversation, and that he might have to help in caring for this new intruder. I may have overdone it. One evening at dinner, two weeks after Pia came home from the hospital, Eric said, "Dad, it isn't half as bad as you said it was going to be."

If you try to understand your older child's worries and resentments from the beginning, respect her feelings, give her as much undivided time and attention as possible, applaud her special strengths and accomplishments, and never, ever compare your children to each other, sibling rivalry need be neither a nightmare nor even inevitable. When your older child fusses, "How come you spend so much time with the baby?" you can say simply that the baby's different and that "When you were little, you needed a lot more time, too." Mention the wonderful things she can do that the baby can't, such as drink from a cup or eat spaghetti. Watch for big sister's moments of agitation, when she takes a little poke at her sister or "forgets" how to do things. These behaviors are little signals that she needs more parent time.

Relish the fact that one child is turning out to be a marvelous athlete and hardworking but average student, while another is particularly kind and gentle with younger children, wins all the spelling bees, is all left feet when it comes to sports. Avoid setting up competitive situations, even small ones like "Let's see who can finish their cereal first." Let your children know that there are so many ways to be successful, so many good things out there to pursue and enjoy.

Sibling attachments can be among the strongest and most rewarding over a lifetime. They have every possibility of turning out splendidly if parents understand there is no way they can love their children exactly the same. There are a myriad of ways to make each child feel respected and valued.

Hitting, Biting, Stealing and Other Parental Nightmares

A two-year-old walks up to a playground friend and bops her on the head with his shovel. In her seven-year-old's jacket, a mother finds some candy she's sure he lifted from the corner store earlier that day. A parent imagines the worst possible diagnosis and prognosis for her child, whom she now suspects is a sociopath in the making. Children's more negative, hostile or aggressive behaviors, especially when they come to the attention of those outside the family, are deeply distressing to parents, who immediately wonder what they've done wrong and what they should do next. I have watched quite sensible parents react to a small child's stealing with angry, emotional outbursts about policemen and going to jail, and to a child's biting behavior by biting the child back. Other sensible parents decide these behaviors are "phases" and watch anxiously for their child to outgrow them.

Neither response is quite right. Parents should take action on their child's aggressive, antisocial behavior, but always in a way that recognizes the underlying feelings going on and that offers emotional support. The child needs to feel responsible for what he's done and take the consequences, even the bad ones. When children assume responsibility for their actions, they learn to be more thoughtful and careful the next time. They begin to understand about rights, their own and others'. The youngster who has incorporated the lesson that it's wrong to hit someone on the head is empowered in his own right not to be hit on the head, to demand that other children be responsible for their own actions that affect others.

A very young child expresses feelings crudely, particularly toward children her own age. The frustrated two-and-a-half-year-old doesn't have the verbal skills to express that frustration and finds a more direct, head-on outlet for her feelings—she chomps down on her playmate's arm or pinches her hard or whacks her on the head with the nearest toy. It's perfectly normal toddler behavior, but socially, it's totally inappropriate, which is the fact that parents must convey. If Mom ignores her daughter's biting, the child thinks that what she's doing has parental approval.

The best approach is to show your disapproval in no uncertain terms through facial expression and tone of voice. I have heard mothers in the playground attempting to persuade their youngsters of the error of their ways by talking in a sweetly reasonable manner: "Now, honey, you know that's not nice. You know we don't bite our friends." It's the rare toddler who is responsive to a logical approach. What a child that age *will* hear is the parent who says "Stop that!" in a loud, even harsh voice. Unless she is used to being yelled at habitually, she will get the point.

Then remove her from the situation immediately and tell her firmly that she cannot play with other children if she's going to bite, pinch or hit. After a reasonably short time, allow her to go back to her playmates. If she misbehaves a second time, remove her once again and keep her away from the other children even longer, to further emphasize the seriousness of her actions. It's often necessary and sensible to control the child's surroundings in this way, in order to minimize her exposure to frustration and keep her away from the scene of the crime, so to speak. It *never* makes sense to bite or hit her back to "show how it feels." That's not only unproductive, it's disrespectful.

But never fail to take action, in the belief that she will "grow out of it" or that she didn't know what she was doing. Hitting or biting or stealing demand a parent's firm, unequivocal response, even though these behaviors rarely indicate any profound, underlying problem.

Of course, some children who steal regularly are troubled children. Generally, delinquent behavior, such as wanton destruction, defacing buildings and harassing strangers, in preadolescent and adolescent children represents the child's desire for attention. That this attention is negative usually means he has received no positive attention, which, in turn, usually means his parents have neglected him. In an indirect way, the child is crying out for help. When treating youngsters who steal or are blatantly delinquent in other ways, I have often found that their delinquency is directed against a neglecting father or, alternatively, a father who is so overbearing that his child never seems to be able to approach his expectations and win his respect and admiration. In either case, the father is unapproachable. The child's delinquent act represents an attempt on his part to get through to his father, even if the child brings punishment on himself and embarrasses his father publicly.

But most often when young children or preadolescents steal it is a misguided adventure or simply a matter of not knowing better. It usually occurs infrequently and is encouraged by peer pressure or the innocent desire to test boundaries. To a large extent, the parent's reaction to stealing determines the child's own reaction and his subsequent concept of himself. In his own mind, he can either become someone who has unwittingly fallen into committing a "misdeed," or be a certified, seasoned criminal with no hope for rehabilitation. To avoid that latter image, the parent should react to an initial stealing episode with real concern and by taking action, but not with excessive punishment or hysterics. It's never a good idea to label the child a crook, either with words or through your attitude toward him, or to then show distrust of everything he does. That approach will crush the child's sense of self-esteem and give him the unfortunate impression that his parents fully expect him to continue his misbehavior.

If your young child shoplifts a small toy or candy bar, confront him about his action; never let it slide "just this once." Say: "You have something that doesn't belong to you and you have to return it. You can't take things that belong to someone else. This is serious. It's against the law. Grown-ups who take other people's things can actually go to jail. Now we'll go together and return this to the store." And do it, right then and there. Say to the storekeeper or clerk, "We got home and found this candy bar, which we didn't pay for, and we want to return it. We know this shouldn't have happened and we're terribly sorry."

Your child will be acutely uncomfortable during this scenario and greatly relieved when it's over, but he'll get a clear message of your disapproval and information he needs about the world at large. At the time he pockets something, he may not realize all the implications of his actions. He needs to hear why it's wrong to steal and what the consequences are. He needs to learn his parent's feeling about honesty and justice. But never pretend he could go to jail, or scare or humiliate him, or mete out severe punishment. He'll miss the point. He may even think deep down, "Gee, stealing things is kind of fun. I'm really getting people excited." Tell him firmly, but with compassion and respect, that what he did is not acceptable behavior; it's against the law; it's not going to win friends; it can give him a bad reputation; it can get him into a whole lot of trouble.

Taking responsibility can, of course, also get a child into trouble. The child may confess to a misdeed and be punished, while other equally guilty children get away with their behavior. Your job is not to go after the other guilty parties, but to commend your youngster for having the courage to come forward and to reinforce the values that led him to do so, all the while letting him know that what he did was wrong and that he has an obligation to make restitution.

The Family Pet

Two years ago, Seymour, our cat of fourteen years, became ill. The veterinarian told us that his kidneys were badly diseased and that he didn't have long to live. My daughter took the next plane out of Milwaukee, where she then lived, and traveled all the way to northern Maine to spend the next week nursing Seymour and staying with him until the end. She had loved him all his life and wanted to care for him until he died. She was a good parent.

I constructed a beautiful box cut from pine wood that had been grown and milled on our property. I sanded it and sealed its seams. When Seymour died, we wrapped him in the blanket he had loved sleeping on, put him gently in the box, and buried him on the side of the hill where he had liked to rest in his last days. In the deep hole we dug, we put small treasures and mementos, including pictures of all of us. We went through a short burial ritual, marked the grave, and put flowers on it. We had lost a member of our family; we needed to express our love.

Some may consider it a bit extreme to treat a pet this way, but to me it's a perfect example of how families demonstrate and perpetuate caring values. Pets need to be regarded as significant members of the family, requiring commitment and responsibility. I think they can help teach children to be responsible. At the same time they are wonderful companions, especially today, when parents are so busy. Children love coming home to a doting cat or dog who doesn't examine them to see if their ears are clean or if they've finished their homework. The pet loves unconditionally.

Pets also give children an opportunity to meet that important need to feel significant in somebody's life. They respond to children, follow them around, treat them with dignity and respect. And children enjoy the feeling of caring for someone smaller and, in a sense, more helpless, of being kind and nurturing. Animals can help children learn human values.

But I believe a great deal of thought and discussion must precede the decision to bring a pet, even a fish, into the family. A clear understanding of rules and responsibilities must be reached. Parents really must use their own discretion to determine if a child is ready to assume that responsibility and if the family schedule and lifestyle can accommodate the pet's needs. I happen to love dogs. I live in New York City, which I also love. I've asked myself, "Would I be able to take a dog out, walk it and give it the exercise it needs? Would I want to clean up the sidewalk after the animal?" I've concluded I would not be able to handle that commitment without compromising both myself and the dog, so I've elected not to have one.

Many parents I have talked to tell me stories about the family pet. Their child begged and pleaded for a little puppy or kitten, promised to take care of all the walking and feeding and cleaning; the parents agreed. Six months, or one year—or maybe even three weeks—after the pet arrived, the child has forgotten all her promises, father is walking the dog and mother is feeding it and taking it to the vet, and both are wondering what went wrong and what to do next.

I'm certainly in favor of attempting a reasoning approach: "This is unfair to us and to your cat. How would you feel if I didn't feed you regularly, or give you a clean bathroom?" Reasoning, however, and nagging are rarely effective. Ideally, the parent will monitor the child's promise on a daily basis and consistently enforce the mutually agreed-upon rules. Once the parent has been drawn into assuming the responsibility of caring for the pet, however, a shock tactic is needed.

Sit down quietly with your child in a setting with no distractions. Let him know you have a very serious matter to deal with and that a very important decision has to be made. Speak calmly and firmly, and if he seems shocked, or even stunned at the businesslike atmosphere, you'll know you are on the right track. Make it clear that the pet is about to be given up for adoption. Explain that you have reached this decision after careful evaluation of the situation and want to place the matter before him to see if he has any other suggestions that would be acceptable to you. Have ready in the back of your mind a suggestion that *is* acceptable—one that gives back to the child the primary responsibility of caring for his pet—and be absolutely prepared to play your part in firmly enforcing this policy. Hopefully, you'll jointly come up with a plan that preserves the integrity of your household and all the family members, including the pet. Of course, you must be prepared to give up the pet if the child says, "You're right. I'm not ready to take care of it."

Because they *are* family members, pets deserve an equal measure of respect, including the funeral ritual at the end of their lives. If you flush the goldfish down the toilet or put the parakeet out with the trash, the child draws the unfortunate conclusion that living things are disposable. Friends who saw our concern over Seymour understood our feelings. They said, "I know how you feel, because when I was little I lost a pet." We all remember.

During his lifetime, one of Seymour's favorite activities was catching mice and moles and small birds. My daughter, Pia, who loves all animals, was always conflicted, unhappy about the birds' fates but understanding of Seymour. "He can't help it," Pia would say. "Those are his instincts." But she would bury the remains of those little victims, putting markers out for every bird and mouse that he caught. We have a hillside full of markers in Maine. At first, she used crosses, but I questioned her as to whether we could assume that was the accurate religious preference. Pia decided that I had a point and developed an ecumenical marker, to pay respect to all religions; Seymour has one now.

Chores and Money

A family is a unit unto itself. The component parts are interrelated and interdependent, and when life is humming smoothly, each part plays a role in the day-to-day business of the unit. The parts include the mundane, unavoidable tasks of doing dishes, vacuuming the carpet, taking out the trash and folding the laundry. It's important for children to share the chores in order to develop a sense of their own capabilities and to gain a sense of importance within the family unit. Even very young children can be expected to keep up with small tasks that are within their range of capabilities. Collecting all the toys to go back into the box at the end of playtime and putting socks in the laundry basket are doable for youngsters and can make them feel helpful. Some families adopt a regimented list of chores doled out to each child, monitored by charts and checklists; it's a workable system as long as the parents remain flexible and willing to reassess the situation from time to time.

When children reach preadolescence and the teenage years, they move into stages of development where, for one thing, their need to be with friends is great and they can feel resentful about housework responsibilities and the time they're required to spend on chores. Parents should respect these feelings and consider their teenagers' dissatisfaction seriously. Let your child know you don't intend to "exploit" him or burden him unfairly. At the same time, remind him that everyone in the family has a role to play in the maintenance of the home. Find out what alternatives your child would suggest, and try to work out some compromise arrangement. You might be surprised to find that the suggested modifications are quite reasonable and perfectly acceptable to you.

Many parents fret about their child's tendency to forget his assigned chores or to leave a messy room and can't resist occasional outbursts about "laziness" and "sloppiness." Children, like most of the rest of us, would rather be doing something else most of the time, but will usually do what they have to after periodic reminders. It never hurts to appeal, when warranted, to their sense of fairness: "Look, we all live here. There are certain things—marketing, basic tidying, meal preparation—that must be done every day. It is really not fair to the rest of us when you don't share in some of the work that needs to be done." This can be said with a flexible and open-minded attitude and a willingness to accept *reasonable* ideas about how he might be of more help. In this way, children not only develop a capacity to compromise, but also learn that parents can be understanding people who respect their feelings and can be dealt with rationally. When parents take a hard line and refuse to listen or to reach mutually satisfactory agreements, the so-called generation gap looms large.

Routine work around the house, however, is not something for which a child should be paid. It's as inappropriate for a parent to pay a child for individual chores as it would be for each member of the family to pay Mom at the end of a meal she has just served. The child who's paid for completing individual tasks will not develop a feeling that her efforts are an integral part of the overall work needed to keep the family going.

Children should have money that is their own, but that money should not be dependent on anything else, other than, perhaps, a change in the family's financial status. A child needs to know that he can count on receiving a set amount of money, paid to him regularly, and that he can spend as he wishes within whatever guidelines he and his parents have agreed upon. Managing even a small amount of his very own money is a wonderful opportunity for a youngster to plan ahead for purchases or to learn about saving by putting some part of each allowance in the bank. But giving money as a reward for work done or school grades received, or withholding it as a punishment, never conveys the right message. Parents who withhold all or part of a child's allowance as punishment for misbehavior often get fast, positive results, but the long-term losses can be significant—the child begins to associate money with love and acceptance, and that can be the beginning of real and lifelong trouble.

Starting with Respect

All these ways of responding to our children's demands for attention and need for guidance essentially grow out of respect for the child—for his individuality, his knowledge, his feelings and personality. Children innately understand when they are being treated respectfully, just as they vividly sense a lack of respect, which is an all-too-common phenomenon. Many people look upon children as nuisances, somewhat inferior human beings who can be talked around, put on hold, or ignored. Disrespect for children is evident in any public place, in restaurants, on the streets, in schools.

For a while when my daughter was very young, she often didn't speak to people who spoke to her. People thought Pia was shy, and she's anything but shy. A neighbor would say hello and ask her questions, and when Pia didn't answer, the person would usually say something like, "What's the matter? Cat got your tongue?" The more they tried to cajole her into talking, the more intently she would look the other way. I always came to Pia's defense, saying, "I guess she doesn't feel like saying hello today. Maybe the next time we meet she'll feel differently." I tried to respect my daughter's feelings and offer a diplomatic explanation that would get this insistent adult off her back. Children don't have to put on little performances for the amusement of adults.

There is no better way to raise respectful children than by respecting them yourself, and by demonstrating qualities of simple politeness and concern for others in small, daily interactions. Children watch us to learn what's important, and they need to learn that just being nice to people is one of those important behaviors. Perhaps you're in line at the grocery store and the person in front of you is rude to the clerk. After that person leaves, you might say to the clerk, "It must be terrible having to put up with people who are rude to you like that. I imagine you get quite a bit of that kind of thing." If a clerk is swamped, I help bag my purchases, saying, "Here, let me help. Why should I stand here doing nothing?" Over the years my children have seen me talk to checkout people, cabdrivers and bus drivers, waitresses and receptionists, and I have noticed that now, as adults, they do the same thing.

In my professional life I have seen so many instances of how respect, or blatant disrespect, influences the mood and outcome of therapeutic practice. Often, physicians teaching medical students on grand rounds in hospital wards will come into a patient's room and act as though they are meeting a gallbladder, not a person, never acknowledging the patient even with a "Hello, I'm Dr. Smith." They just begin their procedures, take out a red pencil and map out the gallbladder, convey their instructions to the students, and then say to the nurse or attendant, "You can take him away now." Students, of course, will pick up such attitudes, just as they'll learn how to use a stethoscope. As a teacher, when I interview a patient in front of a class of medical students, I'm very conscious of that person's dignity and I always thank him for coming. If these students are helped to see patients as human beings with feelings, they will be better doctors.

In medical situations, I urge doctors I am working with to talk to the nurses, bring them into discussions and not dismiss their opinions. Much of the friction and discord in hospitals is due to the fact that nurses have tremendous responsibility and essentially no authority, while most of them have a great deal of medical knowledge and sometimes more experience than the doctors, in certain situations. Understandably, they feel stress and anger when doctors come through and ignore them or talk down to them.

Today, when people say to me, "Your son is a wonderful doctor; he goes out of his way to be considerate," it feels supremely satisfying. And I know that when he becomes a parent, his children will experience the same demonstration of respect for others.

Appropriate dress shows self-respect and respect for others. Children absorb lessons about the importance of appearance when they see family members dress in a clean, attractive manner. When I was in Wichita, Kansas, recently to give a speech, the people who came to hear me arrived in suits and ties and dresses and sat down politely waiting for me to start. I looked out into the audience and said, "I can't help but comment on how nice you all look." I felt honored. Dressing nicely is a way of communicating respect for other people. It's caring, and it's also a powerful influence on feelings of self-esteem.

I worked in state mental hospitals in the early 1950s, a time before the availability of medications to help psychotic people. I remember being particularly impressed by the beauty parlor in one facility; I saw a tremendous change in the female patients who went there. When these women came back with their hair fixed attractively and makeup applied, they walked differently, held themselves straighter, and even spoke more directly, and with authority. Somehow, by changing their images of themselves, they became somewhat different people.

When my son, Eric, was a teenager, he'd often appear for a family evening out dressed in odd-looking clothing. Although I was sometimes startled by his appearance during those challenging years, he was always responsive to a reasonable request and a muted reference to his self-respect. I would say, "You know, Eric, you'd look so much better if you had on a jacket and fresh pair of pants. Wear a jacket as a favor to me and you can always take it off later." And he would.

In all the small ways we speak with kindness to our children, show courtesy to others, present ourselves positively to the world, we demonstrate the powerful value of respect and send out little waves of positive influence that have unseen and untold effect.

We parents, primary role models for our children, should never sit back passively when we see behaviors or attitudes that are mean spirited, hostile, disrespectful or just plain wrong. We can never force children to share our feelings, but we can always express our views, and they will hear. My children and I argue and raise our voices at times, but we are just as likely to put our arms around each other right in the middle of the explosion. It's our way of saying, "I need to get across to you some things that are important to me. I'm not going to make you do this; your life is your own and you can and will do what you want. But you must also know that this is how I feel and this is why I feel that way."

6

The Restructured Family

As a boy, I knew no divorced people among my parents' friends. Divorce was not an option in the event of an emotionally failed marriage for any number of reasons, including the powerful societal commitment to the institution. In recent decades, of course, the belief in an individual's right to personal freedom and happiness certainly has been one of the factors contributing to an increased willingness to end a marriage, to a lessening of the importance of marriage as an institution and to a shift in popular attitudes toward people who publicly acknowledge marital failures.

A survey in 1959 found some two-thirds of the public labeled divorced people as "sick," an opinion only a handful of Americans would share today. In response to a question in the Mellman & Lazarus survey that asked whether a married person who stops loving his or her spouse should probably get divorced or probably try to stay married, about half believed the unhappy couple should try to keep the marriage intact and about half felt they should probably divorce. People are saying, yes, a marriage should be

93

honored and, yes, sometimes it should end. And that understanding certainly has a lot to do with the new definition of family: a group of people, according to three-fourths of the survey respondents, who love and care for each other, who are not necessarily related by blood, marriage or adoption or necessarily people living in the same household.

I think that dramatic statistic reflects an optimistic response to the changing nature of the personal lives we lead today. We're saying that the key family values will not necessarily be fulfilled through the connections of birth or marriage, but that we can seek them out and nurture them among the people we love and care for. And when parents divorce, the values of respect, emotional support and honoring responsibilities are perhaps more desperately important than ever if the children are to thrive.

When a Marriage Ends

The end of a marriage and the dissolution of a family are devastating events. Although there is little social stigma attached to divorce these days, studies have shown that next to the death of a loved one, divorce is the most stressful situation an individual can face. Most people embark on a marriage full of eagerness and promise, anticipating the garnering of life's richest rewards—happiness, companionship, a pleasurable and fulfilling commitment to a home and a family. Marriage promises freedom from loneliness, the pleasant anticipation of shared growth, feelings of completeness and interdependence. When these expectations and high hopes fail, sometimes after months or even years of trying to resolve differences, and it's clear that the marriage is destructive to one or both spouses, the feelings of loss, failure and confusion can be overwhelming. I have counseled patients on the brink of divorce who have felt almost disoriented, uncertain of what to do, literally, in the next hour. Divorce sets up circumstances that are so disorganizing that everyone subjected to them feels overwhelmed and wonders how he or she can make it through. Juxtaposed to looming feelings of sorrow and aloneness—this person I expected to spend my life with is no longer in my life—are a myriad of small worries and decisions to be made: I must buy new furniture, call the lawyer tomorrow, tell friends what's going on. Almost everything that has been stable must be reorganized. And this uncertainty and upheaval leaves the divorcing man or woman in a state of chronic anxiety, subject to periodic attacks of panic, unable to imagine ever feeling settled again.

Undeniably, divorce is one of the most traumatic experiences one can undergo, an event that seems to warrant precious little support from the world. Society has given hearty endorsement to the idea that marriage is the culminating opportunity for growth in people's lives. Marriage traditionally begins with reassuring ceremonies and rituals. But there are no traditional provisions for what happens beyond the breakup of a marriage. Divorce is simply considered evidence of a failed marriage, a failed life. Little wonder it is so painful.

I urge couples considering, and perhaps fearing, divorce to understand that just as marriage is a developmental stage in life, so is divorce for many men and women. Marriages fail for any number of reasons, many of them appropriate to ending a relationship. There is a greater convergence of feelings and values, goals and ideas about what would make both individuals happy at the beginning of the marriage than there will ever be later on. And most likely, neither husband nor wife has revealed—or even may be fully aware of—all his or her expectations of the marriage.

People change. Every day of life brings modifications to an individual's thoughts and feelings. Sometimes marriage partners develop in different directions; emotional needs change as husband or wife experiences success or disappointment in other areas of life, and the implicit contract (You will shore up my confidence; I will be your sounding board) that gave the marriage its early stability shifts or comes undone. Resentments build, hostility develops and love is lost. Some marriages in that stage are held together by mutual distrust or anger; they offer little pleasure to the partners, and the satisfactions of these "love-hate" relationships are, at best, perverse. Most will end, and if the decision to divorce has come after careful examination of problems, frank self-evaluation and the insights that time provides, it is the right one.

I don't believe that with a little counseling all potentially divorcing couples can avoid divorce. I have seen a great deal of family therapy, including many uncomfortable sessions during which participants have been encouraged to "let it all out," and unfortunately a lot of what came out should not have. Husbands and wives in such hothouse situations make statements that they regret and that, once said, color all that follows. Counseling can be effective if each spouse is a willing participant in the process and if neither anticipates a quick fix, or, as in an ad for painkillers, instant relief.

The antidote to the trauma of divorce is love, respect, solid communication and a firm grasp on "family" values.

Is it logical or humanly economical to continue life in an unhappy situation that promises little possibility of improvement in the future? Or is it better to modify the situation by agreeing to divorce? When a divorce results from these circumstances, might it not be more logical to see it as a developmental stage of growth, rather than as a failure? But whether, in fact, it turns out to be a stage of growth for you will depend on whether you are able to put the pain of a failed marriage behind you, learn from what has happened, mobilize your resources and begin the next stage of your life. The best chance of that happening is if you and your spouse make gargantuan efforts to avoid the ventings of spleen that are so tempting and the down-and-dirty tactics that our adversarial legal system so often encourages. Husband and wife must make it possible for each other to come away from the marriage with integrity and self-respect intact, especially if children are involved.

Children of Divorce

Much has been written about "the impact of divorce on children." I believe that children can tell us, more powerfully than any studies, what their true feelings are about this most devastating disruption to family life. I remember two children, in particular, who in separate instances, explained to me what children most hate and fear about their parents' divorce.

One was a seven-year-old girl who was having a terrible reaction to her mother and father's divorce. She was deeply depressed and tearful all the time, and unable to talk to anybody about her unhappiness. Eventually, she confided in me that she believed the divorce was all her fault. One night, when her dad had tucked her into bed, he had asked for a good-night kiss. She had told him, "I don't feel like kissing tonight." She said to me, all these many months later, "That's why he left—because I didn't give him a kiss."

The second child was participating in a television program I moderated on the subject of children and divorce. I had asked, "What is it that is really awful, that you really hate about having divorced parents?" This boy answered, "I hate it when I've been visiting my dad and I come back home and my mother asks me questions like, 'Does he have a girlfriend?' 'What does she look like?' "

Did I cause the divorce? Do I have to take sides against a parent? Those are the two issues that tear children up as they struggle to work out a way to come to terms with their anxiety, confusion and feeling of disruption.

It's never a good idea to keep children in the dark if a divorce is planned or clearly inevitable, because they know, invariably, more than we think. Your child should be told that every attempt was made to work out your problems so that his mom and dad could live happily together. Tell him that as it turned out, you felt you would be happier living apart. Because some children argue this point and insist that their parents should stay together, you may have to emphasize that your decision was made after careful thought and after trying in every way you knew how to work matters out. The child is frequently terrified, believing that if his parents can stop loving each other, they can also stop loving him. Reassure him over and over, if necessary, that "Even though Mom and I are getting divorced, we're not divorcing you. We will both always love you." Let him know that—if this is the case— both of you will continue to see him and take care of him even though he will spend time with each of you separately.

He may fiercely resist the idea of your divorce. Of course, it helps if his mother and father attempt to protect each other's integrity and self-esteem and resist whatever temptation there may be to share their hostilities with the child. But no matter how careful you are in explaining the reasons for your separation, the situation will still be difficult for your child, if for no other reason than that it will probably involve a major change in his living arrangements. He will now have two homes and will not have the experience of seeing his mother and father interact in either positive or negative ways. For some children in some situations, even angry exchanges between his parents may be preferable to no common life at all.

Some children may ask numerous and specific questions about what happened and why. Others may seem to be less curious about the change. All children will be focusing furiously on the concrete elements of what their future lives will be like. Will I have a bed in my dad's new house? How will I get to soccer practice? Where do I go on Christmas? And most will be wondering if something they did caused their parents to divorce.

Young children are egocentric and, especially when very young, feel that they cause most of the events that take place in their lives. Additionally, and unfortunately, most children are often commonly discussed as an issue in the divorce and become the central sticking point of the dispute between the parents. The child is always aware and, if he overhears or is brought in on any such arguments or differences of opinion, naturally considers himself the absolute center of all the painful upheaval in the family.

In your child's fantasy, she wonders if she might have prevented the separation from happening had she done something differently. She may fix on small, isolated instances of what she sees as her own rejection of, or meanness toward, her parents— like the little girl who denied her father a good-night kiss. Grown-ups and their lives can be terribly mysterious to children; although children are acutely aware of the tension and unhappiness, the fine points of cause and effect are beyond their understanding. You must reassure your child that the divorce has taken place because her parents are no longer happy when they live together and are happier being away from each other, but she is *not* the cause and nothing she could have done would have prevented you from divorcing.

A child will sometimes work very, very hard to fix whatever she did "wrong" and to bring her parents together again. All children fantasize about how nice it would be if their parents would get back together. They wish for some magical way to make this happen. That's why it is so important for parents to make very clear to the child, "We made this decision. It's a final decision. And there's nothing you did that made it happen." This at least takes the pressure off the child who feels responsible for ending the marriage—and subsequently, for its repair.

Later, your child has a host of new, difficult feelings to confront. If you are beginning to develop a social life, your child may think you are bringing strangers into his life to take the place of his "lost" parent and he may deeply resent these strangers. Or he may accept them simply because he needs to associate with individuals of his absent parent's gender. In either case, the child sees this new individual as a replacement for his lost parent, one he will accept or resent. This is terribly difficult for a mother or father struggling toward a fresh beginning or attempting to move forward in a happier relationship. You must remember that your child's reaction really has little to do with how he feels about the new friend and mostly with how he feels about the mother or father who is absent.

Divorced parents often worry about the possible dangers involved when a child is exposed to a mother's new boyfriend or a father's new date. You need to realize that seeing his parents dating or involved with someone new creates conflict and anxiety for your child, simply because he wants to have his original parent back and at the same time wants to have "someone" to satisfy the unfulfilled needs in his everyday life. Your child desperately wants a man (or woman) in the home, but accepting this substitute parent feels to him like the equivalent of severing all ties with his biological father or mother. You must not underestimate how severe the anxieties of this choice can be. A child frequently has intense emotional reactions and behaves neurotically when he begins to relate to a newcomer who is taking the place of his real parent.

Parents often ask me about the wisdom of inviting a new companion to sleep overnight. For the child, an overnight guest represents, quite directly, someone taking the place of his absent parent. Consider the child's needs and exercise great discretion. When you begin to date seriously, your child not only has to cope with a substitute for his "lost" parent, but also has to adjust to the shocking reality of a parent who is frequently going off to have fun elsewhere. It may be just too much for your child, who may go as far as to create problems and be so rebellious that you are forced to pay increased attention to him. Jealousy is very common and can be expected even when your child has a strong relationship with and a need for a substitute parent.

If a divorce has occurred in part because one parent has started a relationship with somebody else, there's likely to be a good deal of animosity in the atmosphere and children may feel pressured to hold resentments or to take sides. Children should never be put in a position where they have to make judgments about a parent's behavior. I urge the angry parent to resist the temptation to say, "We're getting divorced because your father ran off with his secretary." The child needs a simple explanation from both parents that says, in simple words, they are dissolving the marriage because things did not work out the way they both wanted.

It's terribly important for the child to be able to retain as much respect for both his mom and dad as possible. If one parent has really done destructive or despicable things, obviously the other parent can't ignore the situation with the child, whitewash the ex-spouse and pretend all is wonderful. The child must be helped to express and understand his own, probably conflicted, feelings.

Resist the urge to use your children as confidantes, or enter into little conspiracies with them, trying to get information about Dad or Mom's new life. Children don't want to talk about these matters and hate being used this way. They also hate to convey messages: "Tell your dad I didn't get the check yet." The messenger role is difficult and embarrassing for a child and it certainly doesn't engender positive feelings about the "delinquent" parent. Divorce is hard enough on a child without getting stuck in the middle.

Ideally, the child of divorced parents gets to spend sufficient and pleasant time with each parent regularly, and husband and wife work together to ensure that all such arrangements happen harmoniously and in consideration of the child's own desires.

All too often, however, the child is angry or terribly confused, in the most basic way, about the new configuration his life has assumed—What does it mean that I'm living at home with my mother all week and that my father comes to pick me up on Saturday and then I stay at his house that night? and who decides that I have to? and why can't I live at Dad's house all the time? Or he is anxious about words he hears that make him feel his parents' unhappiness has to do with *him*.

Listen to the terminology we use when a divorce involves a child or children: parents "fight" for custody in "custody battles"; they "win" custody; are "awarded" custody or have "visitation rights"; the terms imply ownership and suggest that the children are, in a sense, combat trophies. How much better for the children (and the parents) if what is termed custody could instead be called "primary responsibility," such responsibility to be directed to the parent who is best able to provide stability and deal with the day-to-day issues of child raising. The parent who is not directed to assume those particular responsibilities *would* be expected to maintain an active, loving, involved relationship with the child, who has two homes—a "primary residence" and a "secondary residence." That child would not be considered to be "living with" his mother, say, while his father has "visitation rights." In lectures I have given to the American Bar Association and the Association of Matrimonial Lawyers, I have stressed the importance of terminology in escalating or reducing hostility and in promoting respectful long-term relationships among the members of families of divorce. Visitation is so frequently set up arbitrarily and can be manipulated by a vengeful parent, or a parent's "rights" take precedence over any consideration of the child's feelings. Parents frequently speak of "my" weekend or "my" visitation. Really, it is the child's weekend and the child's visitation. The parents are inclined to "own" the child's life, or treat her, in a sense, like a prisoner, and of course the child is resentful.

Children need to feel that their opinions and desires are being given recognition; if they sense they are vulnerable to everybody else's decisions and choices, they feel depressed, helpless and lonely. Certainly, young children can't decide whom they want to live with, but their declared wishes can be listened to or their unspoken feelings—tentative, conflicted, scared—can be acknowledged. The six-year-old who suddenly protests vigorously about going to Dad's for the weekend isn't necessarily saying he doesn't like being with his father. He could be feeling particularly attached to his own bed, or wishing his mom and dad didn't live in different places. Maybe he is feeling a little annoyed about not having his favorite toys and things around when he wants them.

Especially as children grow into the preteen years, their own needs and wishes must be heard. One eight-year-old boy named David began to show intense anger, picked on younger children, and was getting poor reports at school. His divorced father brought him to me to help get to the bottom of the boy's anger and aggressiveness. David had no major objections to the custody arrangement and, in fact, said things were much better now that the divorce was over. But he was very unhappy because he couldn't do many things his friends could do. He couldn't spend a weekend with a friend because his mother insisted it was her weekend to be with him, and over Christmas and school vacations, his time had to be equally divided between his parents.

David actually tried to trade off visitation days, offering to pay his mother back in days if she would let him go on trips and spend time with his friends during "her" days, but she held fast to her "rights." David, understandably, felt manipulated and was furious with his mother: "She doesn't care about me or my feelings. She doesn't respect me. She's only interested in herself." He felt mistreated both by the legal decision that dictated how he would spend his weekends and by his mother's rigid adherence to it.

Although they don't like it, children do understand that people can stop loving each other. But they need to feel they have some effect on the world, some control over their day-to-day lives. They need continuity in their relationships with the people who make them feel important and valued. The transition will never be problem-free, but if the child feels that "I have some say in this," he has a better chance of navigating the changes with his self-esteem intact.

Children of divorce do go through trauma, but it doesn't have to leave them emotionally scarred. Most studies of children and divorce have implied that the divorce caused whatever scars and wounds the children reveal. In reality, many of those scars may have been caused by the *marriage*, by the accumulated tensions and adjustments children experience living in an unhappy home. The divorce in some ways can relieve the pressure and enable people to get on with life and establish positive relationships. It is significant to me that while many of my adult patients have said, "I wish my parents had gotten divorced," I have never had an adult child of divorced parents say to me, "I wish they had stayed together."

While divorce always involves pain, to stay together for the sake of the children is a cliché that, happily, has become outmoded. To stay together after growth stops in a loveless, embittered marriage is far more damaging to the children than is divorce. Over the years, in my practice I have found that children with divorced parents who had made them part of a loving family through a new relationship came away with a more positive attitude about marriage than did those whose battling parents stayed together.

Couples who divorce and then build subsequent lives around the divorce are what I call injustice collectors. They instigate or perpetuate more and more conflict, in an unwillingness or inability to let go of the past and move on. When couples grow apart, there is not necessarily a villain and a victim. But even if a former husband and wife never become buddies, life sits lighter on their children if they achieve a measure of mutual respect and kindness.

Going It Alone: Single Parents and Child Raising

I counseled a woman in her mid thirties, successfully established in a well-paying job, who had, she told me, no particular inclination toward marriage but a fervent wish for a baby. She had picked out the man to father the child, although he was not to be involved in any further aspect of parenthood beyond the act of procreation. Being a methodical person, she was seeking my advice on how she might, at some future point, explain to her child his absent father.

I suggested to her that that was probably among the least pressing of her concerns. I tried to encourage her to do some deep rethinking of her plan. I said, "Under the best of circumstances, with two loving parents and an intact home, taking on the responsibility of parenthood is enormous. Here you will be starting out without a partner to help you, and you're depriving the child of a father. And who will raise the child while you're working?" She had selected a day-care facility, she said.

I urged her to reconsider, saying, "Your first responsibility is to the child, which means at this point you must try to imagine the day-to-day work involved in maintaining yourself *and* a baby.

The physical fatigue alone is overwhelming. You will need a tremendous amount of emotional strength, good family support or good and willing friends. Single parenthood creates financial stress, logistical hassles, and tremendous demands on your time."

She understood all that, she said, and it would all be taken care of. She would proceed with her plan because, she said, "It's my right to have a child." I wished her well. Privately, I thought she might have some startling surprises in store.

Certainly, it is possible for a single man or woman to raise a child successfully, as countless numbers of divorced and widowed mothers and some single fathers are doing right now. And, yes, the potential for happiness and bringing children up with a positive attitude about family life is greater in a happy single-parent home than in the hostile, bitter atmosphere of a bad marriage. But there are almost always hardships, and I don't encourage a single person to elect to raise a baby alone.

It's easy to fantasize about rearing a lovely, happy baby who fits into an already well-organized life. While the fantasy is appealing, the reality is almost always different and the baby's needs are almost always compromised from the start. The presence of a baby, per se, disrupts that organized life. The good job, the lovely apartment and the personal freedom the woman enjoyed prebaby are all affected by the demands of this new, needy person. I urged—unsuccessfully, I think—that very determined mother-to-be to consider making the children of friends and relatives part of her life, inviting them for afternoon adventures or weekend visits, or to volunteer to work with children in her community. Certainly, parenthood is a joy, but for the welfare of the child, every potential parent must enter into it with a hardheaded appreciation of its responsibilities.

Significant numbers of American children of divorce are growing up in single-parent homes. The configurations and special requirements of these restructured families demand that everyone, grown-ups and children, become aware of the practical realities involved in getting through a day. I am a strong supporter of mandatory school programs that educate our youngsters in "home work": preparing meals, caring for the house, attending to the needs of babies and very small children. I call such a program "human survival training." These are good things to know, whatever the life circumstances, but such training is of particular value in the event of divorce. It would provide men and women with a keener knowledge of how to function responsibly as the sole provider or caretaker of the family, which can minimize many of the stresses that people encounter immediately following divorce—because stresses there will be.

As a newly single person, your life has probably taken on an unexpected quality. After living in a conflict-ridden or stifling marriage, it's natural to anticipate that divorce will bring freedom and new opportunities for self-expression. Most of all, you look forward to the tremendous relief from the strains you experienced before. That fantasy of liberation is not totally a fantasy, but it takes time to get there. When the immediate sensation of being liberated wears off, new and different concerns become apparent. Whether you are a man or woman, whether you have primary custody of your children or not, you must be prepared for a period of disorganization.

The friends you and your spouse had during your married life frequently drift away. As a single person, you may have trouble adjusting to being alone at gatherings, and if you include new dates in social events with old friends, you may find a prevailing awkwardness. You may have a wish to meet more people and find that the pattern of your previous social life doesn't lend itself to your new interests. And even as all those highly personal adaptations are taking place, the most important change is happening in the relationship between you and your children.

For the parent with primary custody, usually the mother, the practical daily concerns—getting the children to school or the sitter, picking them up, preparing meals and making sure clean clothes are in the drawer, paying bills and making repairs—can seem overwhelming at times and can certainly cause emotional stress, the feeling of being buried in responsibility. For the parent who does not have primary custody, who probably sees the children only periodically, the financial pressures of maintaining two households may loom large. And many single parents in this situation, usually fathers, are lonely and feel a deep sense of loss of the family atmosphere. One single father said to me, "Even if I see my children one day a week, it's so good to hold on to that little element of family life."

These responsibilities and discontinuities are hard and painful, especially in the early months of single parenthood. The key issue, always, is not to compromise your child's emotional health. It helps enormously to let your child know that even if you can't be with him during the day while you're at work, or won't be able to see him until the weekend, you are thinking of him and would like to be with him. Tell your child that you think of him often during the day, even when you're not together. Telephone regularly. If you can possibly arrange it, see your child in the middle of the day for a brief visit.

Socialize with other single parents; you will probably find it more natural and easier to be with other divorced parents because they have greater understanding of the emotional commitments and responsibilities to the children. A single parent's social life is rarely easy to arrange. While it might be more enjoyable to go out to a movie with friends or to a party, your child may need help with her schoolwork that night or a little additional talk time and attention. Certainly, self-sacrifice and total absorption with the child's concerns at the expense of all personal involvements is not a good idea; for one thing, no child enjoys feeling that she is the sole source of all her parent's pleasures or miseries. But especially in the beginning, as you and your child adjust, inch by inch, to a lifestyle that is possibly radically different in almost all practical emotional ways, her needs must take precedence.

If you are not the custodial parent, avoid the urge to program every moment of your child's visit or your weekend together with one activity after another. Parents who sorely miss their children often use visits to assure themselves of the child's continued affection. Fathers may be tempted to buy the child anything she wants, take her anyplace she feels like going, indulge her with anything she likes to eat. Such overindulgence really serves the parent's need more than the child's. One experienced divorced father claims everyone feels better when he does things *with* the children rather than *for* them; his youngsters especially enjoy it when he plays games with them or reads to them. He deliberately resists buying them a lot of things so they will not view him solely as a provider of material things.

Children are enormously resilient and, in the long run, are usually quite flexible about accepting a mom or dad's new friends into their own lives, even encouraging their parents to make new friends. Ideally, a child wants to see her parents happy with other people, as long as *it does not cause her to feel left out.* For this reason, it's wonderful when single parents, in the course of establishing new social lives, incorporate their children, as appropriately as possible, into their grown-up plans and activities. A child's feeling of belonging to two parents, even though they may now live apart, is the best possible outcome of divorce and single parenthood.

The Blended Household: Stepfamily Issues

One of the most difficult rearrangements that can take place in the aftermath of divorce is the blended or reconstituted family—a marriage between two divorced (or widowed) people who bring children with them and attempt to shape a new family constellation. In my years of practice, I have never seen a blended family that has been wholly successful in resolving the many problems that arise, and I have found that the problems increase when both spouses have children who come to live under the same roof.

It is extremely difficult for these parents, even with a full store of love, energy and determination, to balance their loyalties to their own children, their new spouse and their stepchildren, and to establish mutually acceptable rules and rituals. Conflicts are inevitable: Who gets the bedroom nearest, or farthest, from the parents? Which set of holiday traditions will be followed? Does Mom now have a new last name that's different from her children's? Small, everyday matters—setting the children's bedtimes, for example—become major issues. If one child, or set of children, has a bedtime of nine-thirty and the other set ten-thirty, a compromise of a ten o'clock bedtime will still arouse resentment in the later-bedtime children.

And when the children argue, with each other or with the stepparent, the parent has a dilemma. Does she support her spouse or her own child, or whichever position seems most "fair"? Being fair and judging on the merits and facts of the argument often isn't a winning solution and leads to guilt-making accusations: "How come you're sticking up for him? I'm your kid, he's not."

Guilty feelings invariably interfere with consistency in setting rules or standards of household behavior.

The only harmonious solution I have been able to think of is, unfortunately, highly impractical. Two adults wish to live together but the children aren't so sure they do. Consequently, the parents maintain two households where each lives with his and her own children, and a third place where the parents come together for their couple time and shared intimacies. The next best solution, if it is financially possible, is to move your family into a new home, rather than have one set of children feel intruded upon and the other feel like intruders.

If you are a stepparent or a stepsibling, there is no way you can make yourself love these new relations. Love is earned, an emotion that grows and develops over time and not one that can be summoned on command. I have counseled stepparents who were upset because they were unable to love their spouse's children. They may have felt close to the children, even affectionate, but not loving. I have reassured them that their feelings are perfectly normal, and that while love can't be forced, certainly there can and should be mutual respect. There should be a sense of responsibility for the commitments that assuming the role of stepparent for somebody else's children entails. Patience and realistic expectations make the transition easier.

Don't force the children to act like buddies, or feel you have to take your stepson to the movies twice a week to demonstrate your affection. Give it time and try to understand the child's point of view. A child can feel that loving a stepfather makes her disloyal to her own father. Parents should do everything possible to help the child continue a sustained relationship with the other parent, regardless of any unpleasantness between the grown-ups. The remarriage of a father or mother shouldn't mean that the other biological parent has been replaced.

That's why I encourage children in blended families to refer to "my mom's new husband" or "my dad's new wife," rather than "my stepfather/stepmother," words that stir up associations with old fairy tales and legends in which the stepmother or stepfather is always a figure of evil. We even use the expression "You treat me like a stepchild" to mean "You don't accept me; you are unfair to me." How this new family is "packaged" will influence how its members feel about it.

Ideally, a parent who is planning to remarry after a divorce will not do so immediately. A child has hardly had a chance to adapt herself to the divorce and the new constellation of circumstances, when suddenly she is expected to relate to somebody new, who is psychologically taking the place of one she loves and depends on. At any time, it's never a matter of getting children to *accept* the new situation; it's a matter of understanding and supporting their strong and fully appropriate feelings. And given time—not months, but years—blended families can sometimes do very well, because children dearly love to have a mother and father at home.

7
A World Outside

"Everybody's kid needs some place to go. There are so many people who are working. If I'm home and that child has a problem, I want to be able to say, 'Well, you come to my house. I'll find a way to help you.' All of us, the American people, the whole world—we've got to start looking out for all of the little kids."

I COUNSELED A COUPLE in their thirties, both lawyers, who had a nine-month-old child. They said, "One of us is going to stop working right now because we don't like the signs we're seeing in our baby. We are sure he's missing us somehow." They had made the diagnosis for me. I asked, "What are the signs?" The father said, "He doesn't respond to us very well anymore. He whimpers a lot. The baby's beginning to get detached." And I said, "You're right. Those are the signs of detachment. It becomes too unpleasant for the baby to see his parents go away. Even though they come back, the separation is so painful, the child stops responding." Often, these children become the "good" kids who don't mind if parents go out. And when they stop showing happiness and joy when parents return, the family is in trouble.

Over my years of writing for magazines and books and making speeches and television appearances, I have been accused of making parents feel guilty because I have attributed some of children's poor behavior and emotional troubles to parental neglect. And couples who are not "neglectful" parents, who desperately love their children and work hard to ensure their welfare, assume I am implying that they should be with their youngsters twenty-four hours a day.

I don't believe that is necessary and I realize that, in any case, it is not possible in most contemporary American families, which have had to meet changing economic necessities through long hours of work for both parents or have faced the difficult challenges of single parenthood caused by death or divorce. I am saying it is necessary to spend a significant amount of time with children, especially in their early years, and that certain responsibilities really can't be relegated to others without some loss of connection. Parents really must assume primary responsibility for their children, which means they must assume a good part of the responsibility for children's destructive or disturbed behavior. By the same token, I think parents should be rewarded and given credit for the positive behaviors they help create, and all our social institutions that interact with families should recognize those efforts.

Parenting and Jobs: Managing Time and Guilt

To the young lawyer couple who felt the only solution to their infant's growing detachment was for either husband or wife to stop working, I suggested that they not give up work. "Clearly, your careers are important to each of you, and I know how rewarding work can be. When people ask me how many hours a day I work, I never know, because I can't really say when work ends and other things begin. There is always a phone call to return, or a new project that comes up. And it's enormously rewarding to see the results of your work, of the responsibilities that you've met successfully. But you're right that your child is your first responsibility."

We talked about various options, and they decided it might be possible to create flexible work schedules by using secretarial help in their home. They did subsequently work out such an arrangement, with the mother preparing her work in the morning at home and spending time with her child while a free-lance secretary came in to do typing and other support help.

Such arrangements are not feasible for all working parents, of course, and are never easy in any case. It's next to impossible to get eight hours of work done between nine and five while simultaneously caring for a young child, particularly if it is a type of work that requires intense concentration. But flexible working hours, switching shifts, changing to home-based work are all options that I feel parents of young children owe it to their families to explore. Parents don't need to be with their children every moment of the day, but children do need to feel the presence and responsiveness of their parents for prolonged periods of time in the course of each day, particularly when they are very young.

They need consistency, and they need to feel that they are important in the lives of their parents. If your child spends most of her waking hours with someone other than you, she will understandably be more responsive to that person's pattern of behavior than yours. Certainly, not all mothers should or can stay at home. But I'm hard put to justify turning small children over to other people to raise, because these early disruptions in a child's relationship with parents can have damaging effects later on.

I have listened to many parents in demanding professions express deep regret over the fact that they are leaving their children to go to work, even including envy of the caregiver who will be with their child during the long daytime hours. Many mothers I've spoken with who have been unable or have chosen not to spend considerable amounts of time with their children in the early years feel guilty about having neglected their children. They also feel as if they've been deprived of an important aspect of their own lives by not having been with their children during those very important early months and years. Of late, I have encountered a significant number of parents in my practice who are saying, "I really feel my child needs me and I want to be there with her, so I'm getting off the career track for a while." I find that an encouraging development.

If two parents really enjoy their careers but see their children as first priority, they can take turns giving their professional ambitions a rest. There are ways that motivated working parents, single or married, can meet their responsibility to be available to their children. Personal computers, modems and fax machines all make working from home more manageable than ever. If you can arrange flexible working hours within your company or can find work a short distance from home, you can steal time on breaks and over lunch to spend with your child. If you're married, perhaps one parent could work a shift that would let her stay home in the middle of the day, so the length of time the child is away from both parents is only three or four hours.

Ideally, one parent should be with the child a majority of the day for at least the first three years. After that age, when children have been weaned and have mastered toilet training, when they know what sharing is all about and have developed good, solid attachments to loving parents, they are ready to go out and make connections with a wider world in organized experiences with others.

Child Care . . . Not Day Care

Parents who must work often have no choice but to entrust their children to whatever care they can find and afford. Ideally, a child in the first few years of life should be cared for in his own home by someone who is a responsive, affectionate adult, such as a loving aunt or grandmother. The next most preferable alternative is for the child to be taken care of in a family day-care home, which most typically means a woman nearby who has her own children and has established a small baby-sitting business, taking in a few children of roughly the same age whose parents work during the day. About two-thirds of the children of working parents in this country are looked after in family day-care arrangements, and if the family day-care home is a clean, happy, supportive environment, many children do well. The large institutional day-care centers, I am convinced, offer the least hospitable, least growth-inducing environment for the under-three child.

Children under three years of age generally need a great deal of individualized adult attention. They are not really ready for organized play with other children on a sustained basis, and more often than not, tend to play by themselves, alongside other youngsters their age. Before the age of three, many children tend to be negativistic and openly defiant, grab what they want when they want it. Since they also imitate the behavior of others around them, they frequently become more aggressive and show more destructive behavior if they have been in close contact for long periods of time with other children around two years of age. These youngsters are not really ready for a group kind of situation outside of the home they know and feel comfortable in.

I don't mean to imply that on a child's third birthday he magically turns into a cooperative, trusting, outgoing little human being. It doesn't happen that abruptly, but, in general, three-year-olds show much more cooperative behavior and can benefit psychologically from being in an organized play situation, such as a nursery school, which actually can be a happy and positive experience for the child, one that helps him learn to deal with peer situations. And ideally, this nursery school child would have the benefit of a mom or dad who comes by for half an hour or an hour around lunchtime to give some hugs and kisses, to share some fruit juice and crackers, to watch for a bit as the group plays or settles down for nap time. Parents have asked me if this midday visit isn't disruptive, another small separation for the child, but I have seen children who welcome this opportunity for close, if short, contact with a parent in the middle of the day, beam in anticipation of a parent's arrival, then return to what remains of the afternoon with renewed enthusiasm and assurance. When a parent is able to stop by during the nursery school day, the child feels that his parent is prominent in his life, even if their contact is of short duration. When children spend little time with their parents, no matter how good the quality of the time, the parent's importance in the child's life is substantially diminished. A young child can really make do with less total time with his parents if the intervals of separation are not long.

I'd rather use the words "nursery school" or "preschool" or "playschool" than the words "day-care center," because the term "day-care" places emphasis on the parent's need to have her day taken care of. The term "school" or even "child-care facility" says something about the needs of the child, which is where the focus should be. Even in the words we use to talk about the difficult challenges of raising youngsters in the face of economic necessities that have parents spending long hours away from their children, we should always speak first of what's important to the child.

Still, day-care centers with their many shortcomings are

where many of our youngsters spend their days. For some young-sters, they can provide social stimulation, group play and initial learning activities, which many children would not have even if their mothers were available to care for them. These centers can be beneficial to children whose mothers are extremely overprotective, extremely cautious, and who constantly warn their youngsters of all kinds of potential disasters, such as falling off a swing or tripping when running. These children need relief and some freedom. By the nature of the place, the day-care center provides a freer envi-ronment for those children of well-meaning but overprotective mothers, and children who feel lonely because their parents tend to be indifferent or distracted may enjoy the camaraderie and bustle of a lively day-care center.

Much has been written about how to choose a day-care cen-ter or family day-care home—knowing the proper ratio of chil-dren to caretakers; inspecting for safety and health hazards; checking on toys, nap-time facilities, and much more. All these cautions and precautions are to the good. Parents faced with the always-difficult need to place their young child in day care need all the informed advice they can get.

I would just add that often parents assume that people at a center would not be employed there unless they loved children or were somehow highly qualified, perhaps even more so than the child's parents. This is not always—even not often—true. The day-care center can never replace the family, and the parent needs always to retain the primary responsibility for the child.

Many mothers I have talked to who have very young chil-dren struggle with their need to return to paid employment and their desire to do what is best for their children. Many young mothers have been admirably adept at moving in and out of the labor market as the family's economic needs dictated, returning to what they understood as their primary responsibility—caring for their children—as financial pressures eased. If it is at all feasible, it is always most beneficial for the child if one or the other of his parents can spend some daytime hours with him each day. A coworker at the hospital where I am on staff, a woman with a nine-month-old child, asked me if I thought it would be advisable for her to return to work for three days a week, spending the remaining four with her child. I suggested to her that she might find it more enjoyable, and that it might also be better for her son, if she worked five half days a week and arranged to spend a long block of time in the middle of each day with her child. Such a schedule would represent about the same number of working hours but would give her an opportunity to be with her child on a daily basis.

These arrangements are never easy for a parent to establish, especially in a workplace climate that does little to support parents and families, and makes only minimal accommodations to mothers who must work. Until employers and government policy become more enlightened about the fact that supporting families is both morally right *and* good business practice, parents will have to continue to forge individual ways to work and raise children.

The Caregiver's Role

A friend who returned to work when her daughter was five months old was able, through real financial sacrifice and because of her determination to have her baby cared for in her own home, to hire a daytime baby-sitter. The sitter arrived shortly before the mother left for work and stayed until she came home in the early evening. This young mother described to me her difficult search for a suitable caregiver. She met with several highly recommended "nannys" and felt impressed by the women's seeming expertise, yet at the same time, not entirely comfortable with the potential employees. The last applicant was a young woman from a different culture, with two young children of her own and time and scheduling needs that presented complications. But, my friend said, "We were talking as the baby was asleep in the carriage right between us. And all the time we were talking, this woman's eyes kept looking over at the baby. She reached over a couple of times and stroked the baby's arm with her finger, and then once, almost absentmindedly, gently removed a little bit of my dog's fur that had gotten stuck to the baby's almost nonexistent hair. More than anything she said, this gesture and her sweet, gentle nature convinced me that this was the one."

I thought my friend was trusting a good instinct there. Almost anyone can take care of your baby's physical needs. Her emotional needs are a little more complicated and have the greatest effect on her growing personality. People who are chosen to take care of babies and young children above all must enjoy children. And people who truly enjoy young children aren't overly concerned with neatness and cleanliness, which I have found is often the case with many people promoted as well-trained, experienced and knowledgeable baby nurses. And grandparents, aunts or other relatives who theoretically should be the best qualified to care for the baby during the mother's working day can sometimes be the worst possible caregivers, if they don't really understand their charges, or their "assignment." Sometimes these well-meaning and truly caring relatives are the ones who try to convince new parents that their baby should be allowed to "cry it out" because "crying is good for the lungs," for example, or that picking up a crying baby will only "spoil him." Grandparents, as wonderful as they can be for their grandchildren's lives, often feel compelled to impose certain child-raising ideas on these grandchildren whether their own offspring welcome them or not.

Parents generally have good instincts about the right people to look after their children. Children generally like people who enjoy them and dislike those who don't, and they will respond positively to a caring caregiver. Nobody takes a parent's place in the child's life. Even an infant can distinguish his parent from other caregivers—the way his mother holds him; the way his father sounds and smells. I've talked to working mothers who feel deeply distressed that perhaps they won't be there to watch their baby's first steps or hear her first word. This is understandable. It reassures them when I tell them that the first time *you see* your baby's first step will be almost as exciting and joyous for you *and* your baby as either of you could wish. Mothers who have a real sensitivity to the needs of their youngsters generally have an instinctive good sense about selecting caregivers and usually feel less guilt about missing those special times.

In Chapter 12 I will discuss more fully the issue of child care that works effectively and does not compromise the emotional and psychological needs of children, as most institutionalized day care that I've discussed so far frequently does.

The Big Step: Beginning School

A young mother carefully prepared her five-year-old for the first day of kindergarten. The youngster was not at all sure that he liked the idea of going to "big school," and his mother took time over several weeks before the opening day to explain to her son what he would be doing in kindergarten, when he would leave, when she would pick him up, what he would eat for lunch and what they would do when he came home. They shopped together for new sneakers and a lunch box. The youngster was encouraged to ask any questions he might have; Mom invited a neighbor child, a first-grader who had already conquered kindergarten, over to talk about what it was like. The first day of kindergarten arrived, and the boy walked off into his new classroom with little apparent distress. Mom picked him up at the appointed hour and heard from both the teacher and the child that day one hadn't gone too badly at all. As the mother tucked her son into bed that night, the boy asked, "Mom, about going to school . . . how many times do I have to do it?"

I thought this mother showed great child-raising sensitivity in her response. As they talked, it became clear that although the boy had not minded the first day of school, he also wouldn't have minded not going again. His mother told him that after Friday, just like Dad, he would have the weekend free and they would make a plan to all go to the zoo together. By the second week, the boy was in the swing of things.

Most children are eager to begin school, but for all, it represents the most dramatic separation from home, and the first time they are expected to meet, at least partway, the expectations and demands of a group of strangers. The more children know about what this new world is like, the better they will be able to handle those new scenes. When you prepare your child for school, stick to the concrete facts about what she will be doing there—when she will go, what she will do, when you will pick her up. Talking about these details will give her a clearer view of the whole situation than if you tell her how wonderful school is and how much fun she will have there. One child who had been told repeatedly how much "fun" he would have in school was disappointed after his first day because many of the children around him were crying and asking for their mothers and, as far as he could see, there wasn't much "fun" going on.

The first day or two of school, or even longer, can be disconcerting even if the child is pretty well prepared for what he can expect in this new environment. I like the idea of schools providing the opportunity for parents to stay with their youngsters for a day or even longer as the children get used to the new people and the new routines. Generally, if the school is geared to soothing some of the anxieties your child may encounter, the experience of going to school may be a wonderfully happy one.

Teachers, the Good and the Bad

Any child regards school as if it were a little like his own family . . . and his own family a little like school. Teachers assume a powerfully significant position, then, somewhere just below parents in the child's eyes. In my generation and my parents' generation, teachers were awesome figures whose authority was never challenged, not even by the child's parents. If the child's misbehavior, lack of attention or poor performance was brought to the parents' attention, there was never a question where the fault lay.

Parents today are a great deal more critical of teachers and the educational system, which is probably all to the good. Although the majority of teachers are dedicated, caring professionals, I have observed a fair number who really don't like children, who don't enjoy teaching. I heard a teacher exclaim to a child during a frustrating situation: "I really don't care if you don't learn to read. I get my paycheck at the end of the week anyway." On another occasion, while visiting a school, I listened to a teacher literally screaming at the students. To one child, she said, "Thank God I'm not your parent. I don't know how they put up with you." The child talked back to the teacher and the teacher then ordered him to the principal's office. That child was obviously at a terrible disadvantage trying to present his case over the teacher's claims and attitudes. And above all, however unruly or obnoxious he may have been, that child didn't deserve an emotional bludgeoning.

But nine out of ten teachers I have been fortunate enough to meet are marvelous, inspiring, dedicated professionals who care deeply about the students in their charge and go to extraordinary lengths to get to know each for his or her individual strengths and needs. What concerns me are the handful of teachers—and most likely your child, just as you and I did, will have one or two in the course of her school career—who are insensitive to children and who, consequently, have the potential to cause some real damage to the child's self-esteem. Few influences can make or break a young child as powerfully as can a memorable teacher. I remember wonderful teachers from my own early school years, but just as vividly I remember certain teachers—I can still smell their breath—who were cruel and nasty and intimidating.

There will also be the occasional teacher in your youngster's school life who is simply on a different wavelength, whose own teacherly instincts respond most naturally to the outgoing, openly curious or challengingly argumentative child, while yours is the kind who hangs back and listens and thus is a less overtly appealing student.

It's terribly difficult for the caring parent to know how to respond to her child's obvious dislike of a teacher or to the teacher's report that a child is unresponsive, disruptive or "not performing up to his potential." Parents must be very careful about making judgments without all the facts. When a child is clearly distressed or comes home from school bitterly complaining about a particular teacher's unfairness, it's seldom productive for Mom and Dad to rush off to school with a chip on their shoulders. But it's also not a good idea immediately to assume the child has done something wrong or is in some way deficient.

Children are often referred to me who are having difficulties in school, and I always look first at the school to see just what is happening there. Often there are understandable reasons for a child's behavior—she's afraid of a bully, or a teacher is actually hurtful or intimidating. I recommend to parents who are getting these distressing reports and/or impressions from the school front that they arrange a daytime visit or two. Talk to the principal or to the teacher in question and say frankly, "My son is having some problems in class and it would be helpful to us if I could sit in the back of the room for a day and just watch what goes on; we feel this would give us a better idea of how he can be helped."

If there is no glaring difficulty and if it becomes apparent that your child and this particular teacher just don't mesh very well, let your child know. Try to explain to him that not all teachers are the same, that some are more friendly or more interesting—and interested in *him*—than others. Tell him in so many words that throughout his life, he will encounter and be working with some people he likes, some he doesn't like very much, and some who just don't respond to him very well. It's a hard but necessary lesson for a youngster to learn that some situations are difficult through no fault of his own and that learning to cope with disappointments and unfairness is not a bad skill to acquire. As a parent, you have to demonstrate your respect for the institution and for the teacher, unless there's an overt problem. You need to get some facts—the teacher expects all students not to talk in class; to turn in homework on time; to line up for dismissal at the proper time—and then discuss them with your child in a way that conveys what's expected of him and is not critical of the authority of the teacher. Parents who, in a sense, gang up with their child against the teacher, in the long run undermine the child's attitude toward education. The child gets the feeling that school isn't terribly important because teachers aren't people who command his parents' respect.

But if there is a problem and you have met with the teacher, visited during the classroom day (if possible), and talked the situation over with your child and you are convinced that she is being wronged or ignored because of personality or learning characteristics beyond her control, then it's right to go to bat for your youngster with the school authorities and do whatever it takes to rectify the situation.

Parents tend too quickly to conclude their child is at fault when any adjustment problem occurs, but I've seen many cases in which the school was simply not recognizing the needs of a particular child and not adjusting to his capabilities. So the child makes a "poor adjustment" or seems "unmotivated," when in fact his classroom situation may not induce much motivation or the learning atmosphere is frightening because the teacher is too strict or, perhaps, the child is simply bored by a boring class.

If something is going wrong in the classroom, a parent is at a terrible disadvantage. If you tell the school, "I know my child and I know he's okay," the school's response is most likely,

"You're not facing reality, you're not being responsible." When I'm called in to consult in situations like this, before any action is taken, I always visit the child in the classroom to see what the teacher is talking about. A high percentage of the time, it really is the teacher's problem, or there are extenuating circumstances, such as problems with another child or clique. In most cases, I believe a teacher should just report his observations about a child's "problem" to the child's parents and leave it at that.

Parents tell me that these days many schools are quick to recommend psychological testing, special tutoring or outside counseling for children who don't quite fit the common mold but are in fact often not in any need of such professional scrutiny. I always recommend that parents who have been advised to have their child "tested" thoroughly check out first just what is going on in the classroom and what is shaping the teacher's opinion.

It bothers me that many elementary schools routinely issue reports that grade a child's behavior in terms of whether he is "cooperative," "gets along with others" or "shows effort." Children take reports like this very seriously, and the fact that they are so subjective and are made by someone who sees the child under limited circumstances and from his or her own particular point of view makes the "evaluation" potentially dangerous, or at least very distressing. If there is genuine concern on the part of school staff over a child's character development, a teacher should speak in private with the child and her parents, communicating his impressions of the child's behavior and encouraging everyone to talk about how it might be improved. A sketchily written evaluation of these very personal qualities doesn't allow for much input or feedback by others so crucially involved and really doesn't show much respect for the child's integrity.

Homework: Whose Work?

Schools feel that homework is the child's responsibility, but that parents should see that it gets done, which makes things tough for Mom and Dad. You're expected to encourage your child and offer appropriate assistance, but if you step in and *do* it for him—which all parents are guilty of from time to time when the hour is late, everyone's tired and the work is overdue—you've committed the unpardonable sin.

Unfortunately, a lot of the homework children get is boring and repetitious, probably the main reason they don't like to do it. Ideally, children would receive creative and exciting assignments that they'd be eager to do. Given the reality of the homework situation, it's necessary to set and stick by some clear guidelines and be an active participant with the child, even though the last thing you surely feel like spending any time even thinking about after a long day is long division or French verbs.

Say to your child, "I know you don't enjoy doing homework, but this is not something you have a choice about. The work needs to get done. If you don't get it done, aside from missing out on learning new things, you will get bad grades. And if you get bad grades, you might even have to repeat this grade. Let's sit down and figure out a way you can get your homework done so you'll be on time with your assignments and I won't get frustrated all the time."

And then make a plan, which at its simplest involves establishing a routine and time for doing homework. Be available to help if your child has trouble settling down and getting started. Open the books, sit down and begin work with her. Never, of course, *do* the work for her. If your child is one who announces after fifteen minutes of effort that her homework is all done or that she "did it in school," you might say, "I know you say you've finished and you've done the best you can, but let me help you do some more work." If you know what her courses are, you can test her a bit to find out what she doesn't understand. If she says she knows it all already, say, "Great, let me quiz you on it." And if the results leave something to be desired, say, "Maybe you should brush up on this and we'll try again later." Nagging or threatening always makes things worse, but if you make yourself available to help, demonstrate a method for tackling this unpleasant task and insist gently but firmly that the work get done, you'll show you understand her feelings and you'll help prevent that overwhelming panic a child can feel when studies loom large and long.

I'm not fond of using either rewards or punishments as motivators to get studying accomplished. Certainly, it's a very poor idea to give a child money or a gift for school achievement. By doing so, the parent is removing all the intrinsic value of knowledge and suggesting that education is such an unpalatable business that any child who endures it deserves a present. In somewhat the same way, forbidding TV viewing amounts to a parent's laying down the law in a punitive way, which can have some positive effect in the short run, but really avoids the larger issues of responsibility and commitment to a task. It's best to establish criteria of responsibility when you feel your child is ready to handle it effectively. You can say, "When you learn to use the television more responsibly—that is, after you've completed your homework—you can have free use of it again." Children, just like adults, have to have options in life. An option in this situation is to say, "You can do your homework or not. If you don't do it, your teachers will be displeased, you'll get bad grades and you won't learn. You'll have to make decisions—about watching TV and other things—that affect your work." The problem becomes the child's, and the choice is the child's.

What's in an A? School Grades

There are B students and C students, as well as A students, and over my years as a professor, I find I have most enjoyed the B ones. Students who get all A's are not necessarily the happiest or most successful or even the brightest. In fact, I would go so far as to say that A students frequently are perhaps a bit nerdy, the ones who have not developed social skills or are compulsive achievers who regurgitate information by rote.

Different children learn in different ways, and in today's educational environment, a child can express his individuality yet not score particularly well on standardized tests, for example, which are often multiple-choice or true-or-false questions that basically involve little creative thinking. Both my daughter and I regularly got C's on such exams during our respective school years, but we both tended to do much better on papers and essay tests. Often the students who don't do well at picking a, b or c, or true or false, are the ones who just see too many options and alternatives.

Regarding a child's grades and progress in school, more than one parent has said to me, "As far as I'm concerned, you're either number one or you're at the bottom." These, of course, are the parents who expect perfection from their children, who insist on straight A's, and who often turn their children into obsessive-compulsive or severely anxious youngsters who finally give up—who say, in effect, "There's not much use in trying. I can't be number one all the time and being number two means I'm a failure."

While putting pressure on children is counterproductive, or worse, parents do need to be concerned about how their child is progressing, encouraging him to do his best and being sympathetic to his frustrations and difficulties in school in a nonnagging way. Help out the procrastinator—and many a child is—by reminding him how really delightful it feels to get something onerous done and be free to enjoy his time in whatever way he wants. Procrastinators, for all their blithe "I'll do it later, Dad, I promise," often feel terribly pressured and guilty—"I have to get it done, I've got to do it!" And they're right. Ironically, that emotional pain reduces their energy level, and they start thinking, "I'm too tired to do it, I'll have to do it later," which of course only increases the pressure.

If a child is working at his studies and perhaps just struggling through, a little verbal tea and sympathy every so often is encouraging and shows caring. A parent can say, "I can understand that you're not much enjoying math. I always had trouble with it myself. But it's important to know that sometimes you have to get through things you don't enjoy." And it's wonderful every now and then to say, "I know you've been working hard lately. I've been working hard, too. I think we both deserve to take a break and go out and celebrate together." And then plan something enjoyable to do, just the two of you or as a family, not as a reward but just to let the child know that something positive comes from working hard and doing your best.

But if a child is not doing his work and clearly not learning yet still is passing his courses, something dangerous is going on that calls for a parent's intervention. There are no doubt some practical reasons that pressure schools to promote children from grade to grade without appropriate achievement. Teachers may also think that moving a child along will enhance his motivation and preserve his self-esteem. Unfortunately, this kind of unearned promotion only sends the child a message that "You don't have to take responsibility for your schoolwork because nothing will happen if you don't and no one will care."

If your child is in this critical situation, you might talk with his teacher and say, "I think you should not credit my child for this class, or he should be penalized in some way for not getting his work done and not keeping up with what's going on in class. If he doesn't study and does poorly in his exams, he should fail." For most children, school failure is the direct consequence of not working. If a child is insulated from failure, he has no opportunity to assume the consequences of his actions.

I have often counseled children who are having school problems, and have in some cases pursued a rather dramatic course of discussion. Recently, I suggested to a preteenager, "Look, I think you really should start visiting other schools."

He was caught off guard. "Why should I do that?"

"Because it doesn't look as if you're going to make it where you are now."

"What do you mean?"

I said, "Well, the reason you're here talking with me is because you apparently haven't been doing your work and you're failing your subjects."

He indicated that the problem wasn't that serious, just a matter of getting to a few things he hadn't done "yet."

And I said, "I know, but you have no intention of doing those things. So I think it would be useful to talk about some real possibilities, such as repeating the grade, switching to another school, and establishing new friends."

I wasn't threatening him. I was just taking him by the hand and walking him through the consequences of his neglect. As he thought quite soberly about the fact that he might not be able to move on with his friends, that he might experience some ridicule or even social ostracism, he realized quite vividly how painful those particular consequences would be.

I said, "But you're the key. It's your school, your life and your work. Nobody else can take the responsibility for you." Which is, after all, the most critical truth a child must grasp.

Our society, just by nature of being a market economy, is a competitive one, and competitions are imposed on children all the time, from a parent's earliest "stacking up" of her baby against the one down the street—who's walking first? who knows the most words? School grades, along with Little League games and spelling bees and a host of other activities and situations, are little competitions that children must endure. As inevitable as they are, they tend to foster peer pressure and a generally combative, less cooperative attitude, and in the area of school, all that dilutes some of the real pleasure children have in the simple acquisition of knowledge. Solving problems intellectually, learning, reading and exploring, should be important, intrinsic satisfactions. For a parent, it's terribly critical to remember that success doesn't depend on your child's level of achievement. If he gets straight A's or the lead role in the school play, that's the *child's* success, what he or she has achieved. All a parent needs to do is meet her child's emotional needs at each stage of development and give him a feeling of being a substantial, unique individual, whose talents and skills can be developed to the point where he can function as close to his potential as possible. A child with that kind of support in his corner turns out well. Whether he gets into the "right" college or not, the chances are excellent that he'll be concerned about other people, enjoy solid, mutually supportive friendships, develop a good, intimate relationship with someone and establish a family of his own. That's success.

8

The
Teen Years

"You respect your children, you want your children to respect you. They have to feel they're someone special. That has to be reinforced in the family."

LAST WINTER, some friends invited my wife and me for dinner. I knew they wanted to talk to me about their teenagers who, like many youngsters their age, were enjoying getting a rise out of adults by some benignly irritating actions.

Shortly after we arrived at our friends' home, their thirteen-year-old son came in the door, fresh from building a snowman, wearing jeans that were literally shredded in the front—not just at the knees, but everywhere!—and barely held together by the seams at the bottom and top. The son was clearly making a statement with his attire. As soon as I saw him, I said, "How are you, Jeff? Did you have a nice holiday? I think your pants are fabulous."

Everybody laughed. I said, "You must shop at the same place my daughter does, because she has an identical pair." When I put the clothing issue in that context, it defused the tension and everybody relaxed a little bit—a better alternative all around than, "How can you dress like that? Go put on a different pair of pants for God's sake!" Which of course is exactly what any normal, harried, mystified parent of a teen wants to say.

I happen to love teenagers. I think they're wonderful, fascinating people. But perhaps at no other stage of child raising do parents and their children have more trouble communicating feelings, one of the family values Americans hold most dear, according to the Mellman & Lazarus survey. Letting loved ones know how we feel is often difficult. Interestingly, although respondents to the survey ranked communicating feelings among the top eight family values, they also said they thought their own families didn't necessarily communicate very well. It would seem that in many families, many members have trouble expressing their loving, caring feelings to each other. That's a challenge that can take on new dimensions during the years a child is making the dramatic transition to young adulthood.

The little girl who once came to you with all her troubles, who liked getting hugs and kisses, and longed to please her parents more than anyone in the world, now is remote, nondemonstrative and uncommunicative. And all this is happening just as a parent's own feelings toward her child are becoming more complex and intense—pride in her accomplishments and push toward independence, sadness at the end of her childhood, fear of damaging influences outside the family, frustration over what the parent perceives as her own waning influence and control.

So many parents make certain presumptions about what a normal teenager is or should be, and that leads to most of our problems. Above all, a teenager is engaged in a ferocious internal struggle to be separate and different from Mom and Dad. Appearance is a perfect example of that struggle in action. Fads in clothing and hairstyle catch on quickly among teenagers, part of the statement each teen is making that he's an individual who isn't anything at all like his parents. In their struggle to be individuals, teens, paradoxically, slavishly conform to other individuals—other teens.

If you can accept disreputable clothes in informal situations and show some respect for your child's preferences, it gives you a bit of leverage. When you're going some place nice with your teenager, you can say, "Look, I think those pants are great, but what I'd like you to do tonight is dress up a little bit more." More likely than not, you'll get a "Sure."

And, as far as possible, keep the well-meaning friends and relatives off your teen's case. So many have something to say.

My son now wears a necktie and a jacket, looks extremely well groomed and well shaven. Years ago, when he had long hair, my Aunt Muriel said, repeatedly, "Lee, why don't you do something about Eric's hair?"

I'd say, "Like what?"

"Why don't you have him cut it?"

"What for? He's happy with it. And this is the way kids are wearing their hair these days."

"But it looks terrible."

And I'd tell her, "Well, you tell him that. He might listen to you, but I'm not interested. I'm more interested in what goes on inside his head."

Harass a child about his style of dress or the length of his hair or the depth and hue of her makeup, and the truly important issues get lost in the cross fire. And issues you *will* confront, you and your teenager, during these exciting, challenging, sometimes turbulent years. Recognizing that, with a teenager, appearances are often deceiving—and sometimes unimportant—is a first step in maintaining a base of respect and support.

My thirteen-year-old friend in the shredded jeans did reach out and shake my hand. It makes sense to choose your battles carefully.

Changing Minds, Changing Bodies

A teenager is a human being who is an absolute expert on any topic imaginable, who can take a very strong position on that topic and, within seconds, passionately put forth a diametrically opposed point of view. A teenager has moments of wanting to be on your lap and cuddled, feeling overwhelmed and troubled, and moments of fierce independence. This is normal teenager behavior.

Quite understandably, it's likely to make many parents nervous and anxious. Nervous parents find it difficult to accept these new gangly, socially awkward, sexually motivated creatures who have minds of their own, who crash into things, who have pimples and changing voices and hormones coursing through their bodies that they can't handle.

When my son, Eric, was a young adolescent, I noticed that he was frequently bumping into doorways and knocking forks off the table when he sat down. I finally said, "Eric, I wonder if we need to have you see a neurologist. Your coordination seems to be deteriorating."

He said to me frankly, "I've grown so fast, Dad, that when I walk through a doorway I don't realize that I'm wider than I was before." He understood better than I what was happening to his body.

The changes are so enormous that teenagers often go to their rooms and sleep after school—and parents fret that the child is depressed, or worry that he's possibly suicidal. In fact, the adolescent's metabolism simply can't keep up with the body's growth and he needs to sleep for hours at a time in order to get caught up. And to eat like there's no tomorrow.

While his body is going through this upheaval, his mind and perceptions are constantly shifting focus. His actions sometimes don't seem to make sense. He displays, at times, the logic of a two-year-old.

Driving back from Maine one summer, I said to Eric, who was fifteen at the time, "Why don't we stop and get some shoes for you at one of these shoe outlets along the road." He said sure, fine.

We stopped at one store, looked around, and I pointed out a pair of suitable-looking shoes. "What about these?"

"Yuck."

"Okay, let's forget about them," I said. "See if you find anything else." He couldn't find a pair of shoes that pleased him, so we left. Twenty minutes later, driving along, he suggested we stop at another shoe store we were passing. We walked in, he looked around and then said, "Those are the shoes I want." They were exactly the same shoes he had rejected in the first store.

It is logical for the parent to say, at this point, "I don't understand you. These are the same shoes." But logic doesn't have much to do with it. I realized that they were the same shoes and I said, "Fine, let's take them."

After we had had them wrapped and were on the way out, I said, "Eric, I know exactly why you like these shoes and you didn't like the others." I was ready for him to say, "Why?" He didn't, which frustrated me. But if he'd asked, I would have said, "Because you're twenty minutes older."

The teenager's whole perception changes, sometimes in a matter of minutes. The best way to help her deal with all the changes she's going through is to respect her feelings. And if we're patient about it and don't look for logic and give her options and choices, she will usually make good decisions.

How to Talk Teen

If you make the mistake of looking at teenagers in terms of their size and their voices, you can easily assume that you're dealing with a seasoned adult, someone who has seen a lot of life's realities.

Teenagers have strong feelings and lots of ideas, most of which are radically different from yours. It riles parents, who are in fact seasoned adults, when a teenager takes absolute positions as a self-proclaimed expert and talks down to them as if from vast life experience. Parents are lured into saying things like, "I just don't understand you!" Or worse, "Wait until you're my age" or "Wait until you've really had some experiences—then I'll ask for your opinion." Not surprisingly, such responses, no matter how correct, immediately turn teenagers off. Respect and accept their feelings and ideas as theirs, no matter how wrongheaded those positions may seem to you. Simply affirm that, "I appreciate your views on these things. However, I don't happen to share those views. If you don't see eye-to-eye with me, I can understand that." You can even express some wonderment over how they draw their conclusions, but it should never be in words that demean the child or make fun of her ideas.

Let your teenager tell you a few things and learn what you can—how to program the VCR or make mocha fudge. A parent's respectful acceptance of his teen's remarkable, funny, irritating differences opens the door to a loving and compatible relationship.

That certainly doesn't mean you should keep your own values to yourself. A big part of a teenager's job is to separate from his family. If he's working to rebel against you, he has to know where you stand in order to take a different position.

Many teens, for example, tend to perceive their parents as somehow hypocritical, overly concerned with appearances, and see themselves on the other hand as boldly "honest" and forth-right. When your teenager says, "Oh, come on, you're just wor-ried about what people will think," there's nothing wrong with saying, "Well, I have responsibilities to you and the family. And I *am* concerned with what other people think. It's not going to cause me to compromise my values, but I see nothing wrong with being pleasant or behaving in a manner that makes other people more comfortable with me."

You might also point out from time to time, "You know, some of what you do offends others. Sometimes your manners can be difficult to take. When company is sitting in the living room all dressed up, it doesn't look good when somebody puts his feet up on the table next to the cheese and crackers. I'd like you to think about that a little."

Remember that discussions don't all have to conclude with a winner or loser. You can leave matters with a statement that, "Of course, I understand you feel differently. There's nothing wrong with that. You don't have to feel the way I do, but I need to tell you how I feel."

Teenagers will hear what you're saying.

Many parents I talk to are terribly bothered by their adoles-cent's "back talk." "My teenager has no respect for me," they say. "He doesn't listen. He won't do what I say." Many are genuinely horrified by the language their teens use. "I never talked to my parents that way," they say.

Many contemporary youngsters can be amazingly outspoken and "have a mouth." But the only parents, I believe, who are truly in danger of losing a child's respect are those who challenge a teenager in an autocratic way or those who have ignored or neglected their children from early on. The children of such par-ents will pay back or reflect what has happened to them.

For most of us, though, a teen's back talk is a kind of red flag, a provocative move that requires a deft response if both sides are to come out with feelings and mutual respect intact.

A parent can say, "Look, I really don't appreciate language like that. If you're going to use that kind of language, it's better that you do it at home because people outside the family are going to reject you if you speak that way. But I really don't like it and I find it very difficult having conversations when you talk like that."

Such a response respects the child's right to express himself and at the same time acknowledges the parent's honest reactions.

In a way, playing music at an earsplitting level is another kind of back talk. My daughter's music was often on full blast. I'd say, "I'd love to talk to you, and I always enjoy our conversations. But that music is so loud I can't handle it. If you don't want to turn it down, I have to leave. Come downstairs and I'll talk to you in the living room."

It's very risky to challenge teenagers by stating, "You do it my way or else!" or "You'd better be home by eleven or you're going to be grounded!" or "You don't know what you're talking about!"—all those rejoinders to red-flag behavior that come so quickly to the tip of the tongue. In fact, the "You do it my way or you're out!" approach sets up a real possibility that the child will leave. I've worked with many families of runaways, trying to get the children to come back and trying to restore some communication. Parents who set themselves up as dictators inevitably lose. Ultimatums don't let teens save face or retreat from a tentative position. They dig all of you deeper into the conflict.

If communication has become so damaged and hostilities so high that a teenager says, "I'm leaving," the parent must make a last effort to defuse the situation. She can say, "Then listen—I can't stop you, but it will make me very unhappy. I love you. I worry about you and I'm concerned about you. I wish you wouldn't leave. I know we're having an argument now, but please don't go. If you want to take a walk and think about things, do that. But please know that I care about you."

Certainly, it's tempting at times for harried, frustrated parents to say, "You'll do it because I say so." But if this is a parent's primary way of communicating, he's not teaching his child much other than to obey orders. Apart from the fact that it's unfair, such a dictatorial attitude doesn't prepare the youngster for life's problems.

Occasionally, it's appropriate for parents to issue orders. If the family is rushing to catch a plane to grandma's for the holidays, for example, and you're meeting with teen resistance, you may simply say, "Get going. I don't want to hear any more from you on this. Do it because I'm your parent and I'm insisting on it." But even then, it's best to add, "We can talk about this later," and, later, to put the command in perspective: "At the time, we needed to move quickly and I couldn't listen to your arguments. I was overwhelmed by the time constraints we were under. But I really don't like to order you around."

Negotiating behaviors by discussing each situation on its own merits leads not only to greater peace and harmony, but to a teen's heightened feelings of self-esteem and independence. And that leads to greater compliance.

I don't believe in setting curfews for teenagers, for example. A curfew requires a parent to be a policeman. Especially with older teenagers, you're better off saying, "Where are you going? What do you think is a reasonable time to come home?"

When my children were in their teens, I didn't have a regular hour they had to be home. Together we decided on an appropriate hour for the occasion, and they never stayed out beyond what we had agreed on. My daughter would tell me, for example, that she and two friends were going to a party at school.

And I'd say, "Well, what do you think is fair?"

"How's twelve o'clock?"

And I'd say, "Fine. And if at twelve o'clock the party is still going on and you're having fun, call me, because it might be all right for you to stay longer."

More often than not, she was home early. And she was so unfailingly responsible in living up to the terms of our agreement that in time I found myself saying, "Pia, maybe you better not call me if it's later, because I'll be sound asleep."

My daughter knew that I was asking for time limits and phone calls not because I wanted to restrict her, but because I was concerned about her. The underlying attitude conveyed was, "It's not that I don't trust you. It's just that things can happen. And as a parent, I worry."

Once or twice, I forgot to set a time with her, sending her off with a simple, "Have fun!" and she said, "Well, don't you care about me? We haven't agreed on a time to be home by!"

When a teenager has fought for a later curfew, it's downright humiliating to come home earlier. She may feel she has to stay out late. But most of the time, if children feel a parent has been reasonable, the need to challenge evaporates.

Hormones, Teens and Sex

Teenagers are not sex maniacs, although if you eavesdrop on their conversations with friends, it's easy to believe they have had extensive and remarkable sexual experiences. Most haven't. Certainly, many teens are experimenting with sex earlier than their parents' generation did, but many are not sexually active. I think there is even a shift toward more conservative behavior among teenagers, not just because of the threat of AIDS, but because they seem to be tending not to date on a one-to-one basis as readily as youngsters did a generation ago but to go out in groups and "hang out" together. All are full of the old, familiar questions and anxieties that we adults can easily remember from our own growing-up years.

In many conversations I have had with individual teenagers, the talk has come around to sex. I've asked, "Tell me what you know about this."

And they answer, "I know all about that."

"So tell me all about it."

"Well, I don't have to tell you all about it; I'm sure you know."

And it becomes clear that they don't know too much, really, that their experiences are more limited than they suggest, that there is a good deal of bravado and embarrassment behind the talk, and that, above all, these young people are eager for guidance through what are complex, volatile issues. And that, all appearances and sounds to the contrary, they really would like at least some of that guidance to come from their parents.

The sexual revolution stirred up issues that many, grown-ups and young people alike, didn't quite know how to deal with. During that stage of social evolution, sexuality came to be viewed as a positive thing, something we can and should talk about, and sexual gratification was recognized as an important aspect of life. Such once-taboo issues as birth control and sexually transmitted diseases are openly discussed, which is without question a positive development.

But these social changes were accompanied by a new and open display of provocative materials to a population totally unprepared for it. Young people exposed to these images and ideas really had no role models for how to cope with them responsibly, no rules for how to develop a code of behavior somewhere between total inhibition and blatant sexuality. If anything goes, where do I stop? In the political realm, so-called "profamily" forces have been vocal about what they perceive as the need for sweeping restrictions on everything from pop music to sex education classes in schools. Anybody who acknowledged sexuality as an important part of a young adult's life was considered not "profamily."

The issue, of course, has nothing to do with being "for" or "against" the family. I am profoundly "profamily." And I think sex education is vital, but it must include more than the basic aspects of reproduction. Teenagers need help in understanding and accepting that they are sexual beings, that they do have sexual feelings, and that the challenge is to learn how to express those feelings in a respectful and responsible way.

But what about the birds-and-bees part of sex education? Obviously, the more youngsters are prepared with knowledge about sex and reproduction, the better they are able to manage their sexuality in a way that will avoid pregnancy or disease. But try to start a talk about reproduction with your teen and you will almost surely get the brush-off, perhaps with a half-embarrassed, half-pitying, "Oh, Dad, please! I learned all about that in school."

Don't count on it. Yes, our youngsters today have usually been exposed to school classes in sex education, starting somewhere around fifth grade, and certainly they talk to each other about what they know, or think they know. But despite all the efforts to inform our children about "the facts of life," wild misperceptions prevail. I had a teenager ask me recently, "Can you get pregnant if you have intercourse while you're standing up?" and "Can you get pregnant if you wash yourself out with a Coke?"

Do start a talk. Parents need to convey their own values and feelings about sex, as well as basic information about reproduction—undeniably easier said than done. Because of our own inhibitions, some of us are acutely uncomfortable discussing sexual activity with our children. My generation was on the cusp of the Victorian era. People of my parents' generation actually took the child into the bathroom to tell him about sex; for them, that was the proper context for something dirty and forbidden. Or they'd say, "I'll take you to the doctor and he'll explain it to you."

If you're embarrassed, it's all right to admit it; your kids probably are, too. But the most meaningful sex education takes place in the home, in conversations between a parent and child. Some youngsters will bring up the topic themselves and seek out a parent's guidance. Most will not, and if that's the case, I believe the parent must initiate the talk, no matter how clumsy or awkward he or she feels.

Your teen should know the possible consequences of sexual activity and should know where you stand: "This is what I think you should do, and this is what I think you shouldn't do, but I can't police you." It's always a mistake, in this as in all areas of interaction and negotiation with young people, to issue orders or lay down rules. You cannot *make* a sixteen- or seventeen- or eighteen-year-old do what you wish. You can convey the essential message: "Having sex with another person is a tremendous commitment and responsibility. And you've got to be responsible not only for your own body and your own safety, but also for your partner. Are you ready for that?" And then you can respect his judgment and intelligence to make sound decisions, at least most of the time.

That's the main awareness that a parent must impress upon her child. But there is a wide range of prescriptions for handling the message, and they are influenced by personal values, thoughts and life situations.

Some parents say, absolutely, "I do not think you should have sexual relations until you're married." I encourage people who hold such beliefs to make their feelings known. I see nothing wrong with parents saying, "I believe that you should not have sex until you are in love with somebody and married to him." Whether your teenager will do so is another story, but it's vital to your relationship that he know where you stand.

Young people must also be helped to understand that sexuality is universal and that people of all ages have sexual needs and urges. Many children today are just as squeamish as we ever were about recognizing the adults they know as sexual creatures. I remember when I was a youngster, sitting around with my friends talking about the so-called facts of life, all of us becoming horrified to think that our parents "did it." And acknowledging with a mixture of distaste and fascination that, "Well, mine did it three times anyway, because there are three of us."

A teenager's discomfort in accepting a parent's sexuality will often come to the fore if parents divorce and one or both start to date. If a divorced mother is dating and obviously sexually active with her male friend, her daughter may say, "Well, you don't want me to have sex, but *you're* having sex with someone."

You are the adult. You need not explain your private life to your child. But you can say, "Look, I'm a grown-up. It's a little different. I'm trying to reconstitute my life and reestablish a family, and this is what's happening with me. But you're not at the point in your life where that's appropriate behavior."

Teenagers need—and often want—our help in learning to say no. For some, the pressures to have sex can be extreme. They may try to tell their parents or peers that if they don't get sexually involved they will lose their boyfriend or girlfriend. Their partner expects them to do it. I would urge that youngster to confront her boyfriend. Give her the words to use: "Say, we have plenty of time for that. I like you and I want to keep seeing you, but I'm not comfortable with the idea of having sex. I hope you'll agree." Tell the child that saying no—and having it accepted as a personal decision and not a rejection—can be a test of the strength of a relationship.

My colleague Dr. Sol Gordon has written extensively on this subject, often in amusing ways. I remember his advice to a young teenage girl who wondered what she should do if her boyfriend got aroused—"What if he tells me we have to go through with it," she wanted to know, "because he's so excited that he's in pain?" Dr. Gordon advised, "Tell him you hear footsteps approaching. That will take care of the whole thing." No one should be pressured into sex.

Regarding their teenagers' sex lives, most parents can imagine no more horrifying possibility than an unwanted pregnancy. Unquestionably, all teens, and preteens for that matter, should be fully informed about birth control methods. Whether or not you approve of their being sexually active, it behooves you as a parent to encourage your child to know about birth control, AIDS, venereal diseases, and how to protect themselves from potential sexual hazards.

I think a teenager should always know that you'll be there to help if he or she has trouble. I see nothing wrong with saying: "I know you are involved in a sexual relationship with your boyfriend (or girlfriend). I really don't want there to be a pregnancy, and I don't expect there will be. But if so, don't hide it from me. I'll help you; we'll work it out together."

The youngster should never feel that if she becomes pregnant—or if he is responsible for a girlfriend's pregnancy—she or he must turn to somebody else for advice or help because "I can't let my family know—they'll kill me."

It's good for teens to feel a sense of responsibility for what they've done. But mistakes do happen to human beings, and a young person is often prey to temptations and urges he hasn't the emotional maturity to withstand. Little is gained and much lost when a parent, understandably disappointed or angered, says, in effect, "I told you not to do it and you defied me. I can't help you out of the mess you've gotten yourself into." Compassion and a supportive stance help a teen to make wise decisions.

Drugs and Alcohol

Parents are terrified at the thought their children may be tempted to experiment with drugs or drinking. Of course. Their adored child is suddenly sailing off into uncharted territory. Overnight, it seems, this youngster who was playing with Barbies in her room or was obsessed with major league batting averages and team trades has entered another world, one Mom and Dad have little to do with. She's meeting friends most weekends at the local hangout; he's borrowing the car to go to parties. Even grown-ups who feel fairly secure in their parenting skills and in the solidity of their relationships with their children start to worry about what's going on "out there." My son is a good kid, they say, but aren't there all these temptations and pressures?

There are. And I think parents should expect that teens are going to experiment, or at least toy with the idea of experimentation. The wisest course—the only one, really—is to anticipate that children will be in situations of peer pressure and to prepare them for it, to let them know as objectively as possible what might happen.

But never say: "Don't ever let me catch you high or drunk. If I do, you're grounded for a month." Threats of punishment don't prepare a child for the pressures he'll meet. Threats are not only alienating—they just don't work. Saying "You can't go to parties" or "I won't let you associate with those kids" is merely laying down the law, not providing the resources that will help the child cope.

I talked to my own children about the temptations they would be facing and about what the consequences might be, focusing not on do's and don'ts, but on if's and what-then's? "If you do this, then this is what may result. And if this results, then how will you deal with it?"

The conversation might go like this: "You're starting to go to parties and to spend time with groups of other kids in social situations away from home. And somebody's bound to say, 'Why don't you have a beer? Come on, try it.' And you will feel compelled to drink because you see the other kids doing it.

"I think it would be wise for you not to do it. You'll probably be reluctant to say, 'No thanks.' But don't hesitate to say it. It's not a sign of weakness, it's a sign of strength. However, if you *are* going to taste some beer, have just one and don't drink anything else with it. You don't know how you'll react. It's possible you might get sick or do something foolish." And then explain the hazards of mixing drinks and describe the feelings your child might have that are a signal to stop.

Say: "I encourage you not to try drugs—I can't police you, I'm not going to be there—but you must understand that drugs can make you feel very strange or sort of crazy, and that can be a very scary feeling. Some drugs can affect how your heart beats. Some drugs can get you hooked even after just one try. I love you very much, and I don't want anything to happen to you.

"I realize that your life is your own and you're going to have to make these decisions. But please remember, there's nothing wrong with saying to your friends, 'No, I just don't want to,' and if they tease you, saying, 'Sorry, I'm going. See you later.' "

Some parents will argue that to say, "I don't want you to drink, but if you do, don't drive" is giving a mixed message or encouraging bad behavior. I disagree. It's acknowledging the reality that a child will almost inevitably face difficult situations and pressures to experiment and may succumb to these pressures. We teach our five-year-olds that if they cross the street against the light, they may get hurt. But we do tell them *how* to get across the street. No parent says, "I don't want them to get killed so I'm not going to show them how to go across the street at all."

Teens and Suicide

Suicide is one of the top two causes of death in the teenage population. Without any doubt, these young people consider life not worth living. They feel unloved. They feel that no matter what they do, nothing will happen that will provide them with any satisfaction.

Some suicides I am aware of have been teenagers whose parents set incredibly high standards for them. No matter what these children did, no matter what their achievements, they were unable to garner their parents' love, support and respect. In my counseling work I have found that these are parents who paid attention to their children only when they got into trouble.

I worked with a family made up of a fifteen-year-old girl; her father, a doctor; and her mother, who devoted her life to her daughter. The girl was an excellent academic student and was training in one of the major ballet schools with, according to her instructors, a great dancing career ahead of her. The problem, as the parents presented it, was that their daughter didn't appreciate the sacrifices they had made and the opportunities she had. They disapproved of her friends, her desire to wear makeup and currently fashionable clothes, her unwillingness to "buckle down" to her dance studies and her inability to see that "she has to make sacrifices now to have a wonderful career later on."

When I saw the daughter alone, she was depressed, quiet, on the verge of tears. After we had talked for a while, I asked, "How do you feel about life?" She said, "I don't feel life is worth living. I've thought of killing myself."

This was not a functional family. These were parents who did not respect their child's needs or support her feelings, who sought the satisfaction of public acclaim at the cost of their daughter's life. Only after I was able to persuade them that their child's unhappiness was, literally, a matter of life or death did they begin to see her as an individual separate from themselves and desperately in need of their understanding and love.

But the child at risk for suicide is not often so easily iden-
tifiable. Suicide, distressingly, is not that predictable. Impulses,
frequently intensified by drugs or alcohol, can be a factor. Drugs
alter a teenager's perception of reality. The child may develop
the distorted notion that "They'll be sorry after I'm gone" and
act self-destructively, unable to weigh the consideration that he
won't be around to enjoy the remorse and pain he wants others
to feel. Life circumstances, depression, psychiatric illness and, I
believe, perinatal influences can also heighten the risk of suicide.
But in many cases, there is little clinical depression. The child
does not *appear* to be so unhappy. About many of these children, people will say, "He's the last kid in the world I ever
thought would have committed suicide. He seemed just fine.
Everything was okay."

Obviously, that youngster was struggling with problems and
feelings he didn't express or even show. But almost always the
teenager at risk for suicide feels alienated and unloved. He feels
that nobody cares, nobody understands, nobody is listening.

It's horrifying when a young person says, "I want to die" or
"I'm going to kill myself." Instinctively, the adult says, "How
can you talk like that? You're young, you have your whole life
ahead of you. Look at the wonderful school you go to, your nice
clothes. You've got a great car." Or: "You don't mean that. You
shouldn't say those things. Everybody gets depressed once in a
while. You'll be over it by tomorrow."

Such responses are human and very understandable. The
parent or other adult wants only to cajole the child out of his pain.
But the message sent is: "Don't tell me how you feel. I can't deal
with your discomfort."

What the desperately unhappy child needs to know is that
another person acknowledges the reality of her difficult feelings.
She needs to hear: "That's terrible. If you're talking about killing
yourself, you must be feeling miserable. It upsets me to think that
your life is so difficult. I want to get help for you so you can feel
that life is worth living. Together we're going to find help."

Then the child feels someone understands.

Everybody needs to feel significant in the life of someone
else. That, rather than depression, is the key variable in suicide.
Often the young person at risk has come to believe there is no one
who loves him, no one who really cares about him. He feels that

what he does makes no difference in the world. Change can begin the minute he feels your love.

Friendships

One Sunday afternoon when my son, Eric, was a teenager, we were walking down the street on our way to a restaurant for brunch, when he said, "Uh-oh."

"What's the matter?"

"Dad, some of my friends are coming in our direction and I really don't want to be seen with you."

I said, "I'll cross the street then."

And Eric said, "Oh, don't do that. It'll be all right."

As we approached his friends and he started to talk, I stepped back a bit. Eric introduced me, but I tried to make the scene more comfortable by smiling, saying hello and then acting invisible. I could understand how he felt. Sometimes it's not cool to be seen in public with your parents, particularly on a weekend.

During these growing years, parents are *there*, the given. Increasingly, friends are the people with and against whom the teenager tests his skills and courage, forges a sense of himself as a social creature, measures the impact he has on the world at large and adjusts to acceptance or rejection. Never undervalue the importance of a child's friend. And, as far as you can, open your heart and your home to them.

As they were growing up, my house was open to Eric and Pia's friends. My attitude was, "I welcome you. I like to see you here. I expect you not to do anything here that I wouldn't do." And their friends felt safe in our home, they felt accepted, and so they spent a lot of time there. Many of those people are still part of my children's lives. Eric has friends who go all the way back to nursery school; Pia does, as well. She writes to them and works hard at maintaining connections. In the summer, they often visited us in Maine and joined us on holidays.

During my recent illness, I received many get-well cards and caring letters from these young people, and some let me know how much Eric and Pia worried about me while I was hospitalized, something my children didn't tell me for fear of my worrying about *their* worrying. Some of my children's friends called to tell me they wished me well, and they thanked me for those times we shared in the past. Today, if my wife and I are going out to dinner, if my children are on the scene they'll say, "Can we come along? I've got Richard and Mike with me." And I'll say, "Bring them along." Or one will say, "I've got to meet Elizabeth later," and I'll say, "Have her meet us at the restaurant."

I want to know these young people. I want them to feel comfortable with me. They are part of my children's family. And I think it's wonderful that my son and daughter have close ties not only with their friends, but with their friends' families. These extended families of friends provide an extra safety net of support.

It's common for teenagers to find it harder to talk about certain stressful feelings or situations with their own parents than with a good friend's parents. And sometimes you hear things from your children's friends that your children wouldn't tell you. That is as it should be. When adults respect all the young people in their lives as individuals worth knowing and listening to, everybody gains.

Not every friendship will be a delight. If you don't like some of your children's friends, respect their choices, unless the association seems potentially dangerous or one that will lead to trouble. You can always let a child know in a tactful way how you feel about the friend. At times, I have said to my son or daughter something like, "You know, I'm not comfortable with Alison. I know you feel differently, but I just want you to know my feelings. Please be careful that she's not the kind of person who's taking advantage of you." I have never said, "I don't want you to bring that person here." I have tried to communicate my feelings and thoughts on what the possible consequences of maintaining that friendship might be. Then I've let it run its course.

One of my son's best friends is someone I find impolite and crude. My son says, "I know he can be a little obnoxious but he's a good friend to me. You don't know him the way I do."

I say, "You're right, I don't. I respect your feelings."

And I do. I'm not particularly fond of this friend, and I think he knows it. But we have civil conversations and I sometimes joke to Eric that this particular friend of his is not my favorite person. We understand each other.

It's always a mistake to attempt to control a teenager's social interactions. The best we can do is share our feelings and accept the reality of different tastes, different opinions and different judgments.

9

Grandparents and Other Strangers

"My grandmother lived with me for a while. I remember one night when I sat down with her at nine o'clock and we talked until four in the morning about World War I, World War II and about her growing up. I learned as much that one night as I did in a whole year of school."

A FRIEND DESCRIBED to me a typical Fourth of July gathering at his parents' suburban home, a tradition for his large, far-flung family: "Somebody drives out to New Jersey to pick up two unmarried aunts whom nobody sees or hears from the rest of the year, and who sit grinning but not saying anything for the rest of the day, and then, of course, have to be driven back. My wife and I can't stand her brother's second wife, who holds forth a lot on her world travels and other boring subjects, so we try to avoid her and also do a lot of surreptitious poking each other in the ribs and rolling our eyes about this truly obnoxious woman.

"My father has a few Bloody Marys and eventually insists on playing—and singing along with!—*The Clancy Brothers in Concert.* Our usually shy, mild-mannered son turns into a wild man with his cousins, which it takes him a few days to come down from, and our teenager insists on reading her book and acting bored. My sister brings a date, never the same one, who usually turns out to be a muscular fellow who keeps trying to talk to me about football. It's pretty awful . . . and when it's over, we absolutely love it!"

I told him his family sounded perfectly normal and their annual gathering, par for the course.

Family Relations . . . for Better or Worse

As we all know, you can pick your friends but you cannot pick your relatives. As earnestly as I believe in the pleasures and the importance of family life, I have no delusions that families are not the source of a great deal of frustration and problems also— for some people, habitually and chronically so; for all individuals, at least occasionally so. It would never have been necessary to invent family therapy if family life was by definition all pleasure. In fact, statistics on violence indicate that violence occurs more frequently within the family than anyplace else. A lot of hazards exist in families.

But statistics also show that people who are married and who have children are healthier and live longer than people who are alone and isolated. Frustration with your family may make you want to scream, but it also challenges you to learn to be more diplomatic, to find ways of minimizing the frustrations and stresses, to learn the hard but worthwhile lessons of patience and tolerance.

Those of us struggling with the day-to-day problems of family life assume we're abnormal, even unique, very much as all new parents whose babies wake in the middle of the night think that everyone else's child is peacefully dreaming and theirs is the one infant in America who is up screaming at three in the morning. People who may be alienated from older parents or find the unavoidable interactions with adult siblings or other relatives intensely irritating and seemingly not worth the trouble are by no means alone. We have put to bed the Norman Rockwell stereotype of family as quaint and unrealistic, but many of us are certain the people down the hall or the family across the street know something we don't know and are able to maintain family ties that are free of friction and animosities. As a psychologist who has counseled many families over the years, I can attest to the fact that even the most ideal-seeming families—the cute, accomplished children and the parents with that serene, trouble-free look—often harbor many, many problems.

Americans indicated in the Mellman & Lazarus survey that one of the most important family values was respecting other people for who they are. Paradoxically, perhaps, that kind of acceptance of differences can be most difficult with family members, the people who know us better than anyone, the people we sometimes feel we can't live with and can't live without. Among the factors that contribute to the bumpiness of family life is the shifting nature and ranking distinctions that exist among all bound-by-blood relationships. The principles of group dynamics apply to families. Some individuals within the group have greater influence than others. Certain people are assigned a leadership role, and tend to set the tone for everything from casual conversation to how major decisions are reached. If a central relative, someone who made things happen in the family, moves away or dies, that change creates a shake-up in family dynamics and forces changes in the communication process. Said one man in the survey, "My father passed away in 1982 . . . it's just not the same. He was the person who held the family together. It seems like after he was gone, everybody went their own little ways."

Siblings who were close as children may find their coming together as adults within the family uncomfortable or even painful, if one has achieved measures of success and happiness that have eluded the other. Or siblings who drifted apart in young adulthood and may even have lost touch join forces and tap old stores of love and affection when parents become ill and in need of help. In some families, most members by mutual consent don't see each other often, maintain a polite distance and don't really communicate, but that dynamic may change when something goes awry in the family sense. Bad news—or extremely good news—will cause people to come together suddenly. And sometimes just a casual meeting, or a pro forma family reunion, can reawaken a sudden nostalgia that leads to the feeling that "It's a shame we haven't seen each other for so long. Let's not let that happen again."

And of course, as we get older we often long for people who have drifted away or the people we have neglected. We want to share memories with the people who were there.

Many single adults may be thinking, "I don't see what this family business has to do with me. My family was never a particularly happy one. My major focus as a teenager was how, and how soon, I could arrange to get out on my own. I've made a life for myself and at this point I don't need people putting me down or telling me what I should be doing."

I have spoken to many single people who feel this way, often with real justification. Some young adults find they are constantly battling with an overbearing mother or father, and are only able to grow emotionally and professionally by establishing their independence. Some must extricate themselves to avoid being overwhelmed by a seriously dysfunctional family.

In recent decades, too, we have seen emerge the attitude that parents are the source of everyone's problems. Many people in the 1950s and 1960s went into therapy and were encouraged by standard psychotherapeutic techniques to explore old grievances and parental failings. This cultural trend influenced our attitudes about family, undermining the tradition of respect for parents, whatever their shortcomings.

This modern quest for independence and individuality has had undeniably good effects for many individuals, but I believe it has tragic consequences if one result is isolation from family. I have counseled many people who did extricate themselves from difficult families or who neglected or avoided trying to establish a close adult relationship with a parent. Always, their need for connections was intense, a need they were not always able to acknowledge. Some patients I have worked with had had a chance to reconcile with estranged parents, and didn't. When a parent died, often the precipitating event that brought the person to seek professional help, there was enormous remorse and grief, and profound feelings of loss. I have heard again and again, "I wish I could have gotten my father to accept me" or "I wish I could have told my mother how much I loved her, but we never got over that argument we had." In researching my book about fathers and sons, that sentiment resounded throughout many interviews I conducted: "My dad was sick, and I feel terrible that I didn't get to see him before he died. I wanted to tell him how much I loved him. I would have liked him to know that."

If you are estranged from your family, perhaps you would like to try to connect again but don't know quite what to do or fear that taking the risk will leave you vulnerable to further hurt. I encourage you to try. Call your dad and say, "I love you, you know," or, if expressions of love in such a forthright way have never been easy between you, call and talk about whether the Dodgers have a shot at the pennant or what's going wrong with your car and say at the end, "I just wanted to talk to you again." If talking is too difficult, write your mother a letter explaining some of your feelings.

Don't waste time, and don't feel it's necessary to retrace steps or get across your understanding of what went wrong. Just find a way to communicate, if not in so many words, "I love you, I need you. And whatever has happened in the past, let's try to transcend those difficulties."

Perhaps family members did something you find quite unforgivable, and the idea of going back and excusing those hurts and failings seems unpalatable or even impossible. I'm not sure forgiveness is always a prerequisite for a new beginning. It's also possible to find the strength to reestablish contact with parents or other relatives by making a personal decision to turn to a new chapter and start over. You may still feel old hurts and resentments, recognizing unchanging differences of opinion, but decide not to allow those pains and resentments to lead to perpetual alienation and isolation. Even imperfect family ties can enhance life and provide satisfactions.

So many people who long to mend family estrangements falter at the first step, feeling, "If I give them an inch, they will take a mile—and we will be back to the same old bad stuff all over again." A patient told me, "All my life, they meddled in my affairs, told me how to live, and if I start talking to them now, they will again." It's a reasonable concern, but not a solid justification for backing away from involvements with those who are, for better or worse, closest to us in life. These are common family problems. People meddle. It is possible to learn how to deal with that.

Set limits. You can politely sidestep intrusive queries and pushy suggestions, or even simply say, "Look, I consider what you're doing to be meddling in my life and I don't like it. These are not matters for you to judge. I like our time together and want us to stay in contact, but there will have to be some areas of my life that are off limits." No one benefits if you passively let upsetting things continue to happen, and especially if you simply walk away.

Some of the frustrations in families have to do with character disorders. Some relatives are, simply, obnoxious, or always angry or negative almost to a pathological degree; anyone immersed in the rich broth of family life must learn to deal with his share of them. Sometimes the course of wisdom is to try to avoid these individuals, and other times it's necessary to face the disagreeable ones head on and pull no punches. I see nothing wrong with saying, "You know, you're very unpleasant to be with when you do that," or, "It's too bad that you always feel a need to put down other people. Frankly, I don't like listening to it."

Sometimes politeness is the largest measure of kindness and respect a child is able to give, if demonstrative love and affection are not possible. A friend talked to me about his relationships with his mother and father, both in their late eighties. Over the years, parents and son had never quite understood each other, often disappointed each other. His parents' rather rigid, conservative outlook had meant that there were many areas of his own life my friend was unable to share. My friend told me, "There is a small window between us. There are perhaps half a dozen things we can talk about amicably, without tension—their garden, their health, my job. Mostly, I listen. I have learned that if I talk about certain things going on in my life, they do not hear or become agitated or upset, so I avoid those topics. I feel we've achieved a kind of communication that is pleasurable and comforting for them, and I'm happy to give them that."

Parents who do things you don't like or can't respect are still your parents. They are people who have made certain sacrifices for you and, unless they were literally harmful or abusive toward you, they should be viewed with tolerance. One can demonstrate respect in so many small ways, that involve neither much time nor any real betrayal of self. Speak politely; help them finish a chore or locate information; celebrate in small ways; be responsive to their feelings; listen if they want to talk. Defer to reasonable wishes, bend a bit, do what makes them happy, simply because these are the people who have been the authorities in your life.

Showing respect in whatever ways you can assures you that after your parents have died, you will have the satisfaction that comes with knowing "I did the most I could for them. They had their shortcomings, but they were my parents and I showed respect for them." Giving parents some degree of respect also helps you deal with relationships more objectively than if you simply cut all ties, which can lead to guilt and remorse that is difficult to resolve. And an open display of disdain for your parents will be glaringly obvious to your children.

Some people feel that the true mark of emancipation and independence is to be freed of all commitments that have been imposed by life circumstances. Individuals who aspired to that kind of freedom over the recent years of rabid individualism often ended in a whirl of group therapies, communes and disposable relationships, trying to make connections and gain insight into themselves. What they really needed was family, the people who, as the saying goes, have to take you in when you show up at the door in the middle of the night. Those are the people who, in the long run, are usually most available to listen, to guide, to cry with. Every one of us needs them, because they are what gives us the strength to withstand the stresses of life.

The Third Generation: Grandparents and Children

Some schoolchildren I know have been, at some point, given the wonderful assignment to interview a grandparent or other older relative, going back all the way through their lives, asking questions, tape-recording the conversation and copying it out, perhaps collecting family pictures and putting together a document of that person's life, for example, "Grandma's History." My daughter once conducted such an interview with a great-aunt who was in her eighties. Pia started out by asking, "Tell me, Aunt Muriel, do you remember when you and Uncle Paul fell in love? Do you remember where it was and how you felt?"

Muriel beamed and said, "Yes, I do," and she recalled and shared those long-ago experiences with Pia. When Pia asked, "How did you feel about school?" Muriel said, "You promise you won't tell? I just hated school!" Muriel and her ten-year-old grandniece spent a wonderful day talking, laughing and remembering what it was like "back then." When Muriel ultimately entered a nursing home, she brought Pia's little book, pictures and story, and showed it to everyone who would look, saying proudly, "My grandniece wrote this book about me!"

And Pia learned not only a lot about Aunt Muriel's life, but some very practical skills. For this assignment, Pia was a journalist, a writer, a social scientist and an anthropologist in the process of connecting old times and new. She learned how to plan and carry out a project, and that she could bring out fascinating memories and strong emotions in another person.

Grandparents hold a unique position in your child's life. They're usually bursting with pride in a grandchild, demonstrative and affectionate, and they relish the opportunity to relive their own experiences with their own children and, most critically, to withdraw from the scene whenever the going gets rough, turning the less pleasant tasks of child rearing over to the primary partners. Many fully believe they have earned the right to indulge their grandchildren and bask in the admiration with which the happy youngsters acknowledge that indulgence. And your child, of course, loves every minute of it.

This little mutual admiration society is one that parents sometimes view with bemusement, perplexity or irritation, but it is to everyone's benefit if this special relationship is encouraged. Grandparents have a vital role in transmitting family values and rituals, and they give children a feeling of continuity with the past and their distinctive heritage, a gift the grandchild most fully appreciates as he grows older. I have heard many adults say with some wistfulness, "I wish I had talked to my grandparents more about their early lives—where they came from, how they lived, what my great-grandparents were like."

It's important, too, for young children to know people of different ages and understand the kinds of problems and reactions older people have. Your child may be surprised, for example, when he finds that Grandma is, without showing some discomfort, unable to get down on all fours to play a game with him. Seeing this gives your child some understanding of the aging process and the differences between people of different ages, important lessons to learn in a culture in which children and older people are often isolated from each other. I think grandparents also offer an opportunity to teach children about life's inconsistencies: "We don't have to do everything the way Grandma and Grandpa do." You can show your child that you are an individual with your own ideas and values, and that even though you love and respect Grandma and Grandpa, you don't necessarily agree with everything they say or want to do.

Most children remember with great intensity the happy emotions and pleasant times grandparents have shared with them— but not all. Visiting grandparents can sometimes be a bit dull, particularly if they are in a nursing home. Children may need a little help in understanding that the purpose of visiting Grandpa is not necessarily for the pleasure or the enjoyable conversation. It's a way of keeping him involved in the family.

You might say, "I know that you are bored when we visit Grandpa, and he does repeat himself sometimes. But Grandpa is a great person. He had a difficult and interesting life when he was younger. He and Grandma worked hard to raise me, and he loves you very much. And, you know, someday I may be like he is now. You may be that way someday.

"Our visits make Grandpa feel cared about. He likes to get pictures or cookies we've made, and to see how you've grown and changed. That's very important to him."

Sometimes, of course, grandparents go a little too far, indulging the child with treats or freedoms against some expressed wishes of her parents, offering unsolicited advice about how to raise children or run a home, entering into little conspiracies with the grandchildren—"Just don't tell your mother and father that I've given you this candy." Some may feel rather self-righteous about the way they chose to live and what they've accomplished. Some may become more outspoken or inflexible as they age and find it increasingly difficult to adjust to small changes of plan, new family friends, or different ways of doing familiar things.

It's perfectly appropriate for you, as a parent, to set limits on your own parents regarding your children and other matters that have to do with your immediate family. There's nothing wrong with raising your children differently from the way your parents would like. And you aren't obliged to give reasons, to either the older or the younger generation.

When your child comes home and says, "But Grandma lets

me jump up and down on *her* living room couch," you can simply make it clear that you don't approve of jumping on the couch: "If she wants to let you jump in her house, that's all right. But you are not allowed to do it here." If you are aware that a day with the grandparents has been an ice-cream-and-candy orgy, tell your child, "While Grandma and Grandpa give you whatever you want, I don't want you to get the idea that I will, too."

You are not being cruel, and your child will not interpret it that way, either. He does learn very quickly to exploit the indulgent attitude of his grandparents and at the same time, often respects you more if you do not compete with them to see who can ingratiate himself fastest and furthest. Maintain your discipline and your values. Show your child that you will not be conned into doing what his grandparents do. I might add that I don't think grandparents really want to "spoil" their grandchildren or cause friction at home. I think they simply enjoy having the advantages of parenthood without the disadvantages.

For the most part, the particulars of a grandparent's inappropriate indulgence are harmless or not terribly important. If you're not happy about your child eating junk food and know she *does* when she's at Grandma's for an afternoon, it makes sense to ask yourself if any real harm is being done. On the other hand, if you have expressed to your parents strong and firm attitudes you have about what your child should not have or be allowed to do, and if her grandparents turn around and give or allow what you have prohibited, they are plainly and simply undermining your relationship with your child.

Situations so potentially damaging can usually be avoided if there is communication among all involved. The crucial point to bear in mind is that you have to be acknowledged by your parents as primarily responsible for your child. The moment any other figure poaches on your prime responsibility, problems begin to develop. If your parents have consistently overridden your expressed wishes, it's time for a serious talk, which may be difficult. Let them know you must insist they follow your rules about what your child can and cannot do while she is with them, suggest you work together to select gifts or food or activities that all sides will feel good about, and say you feel strongly about the need for better communication and cooperation.

Most grandparents are perfectly capable of adopting a little discretion in exercising their advice-giving or grandchild-indulging roles. These are just part of ordinary family dynamics that make life a little more complex and frustrating. But grandparents don't exist to cause conflicts and headaches, and youngsters should have the chance to share in their lives.

10

Insidious Influences

"With the Cosbys on TV, is one of them taking a drag on a cigarette really a problem that you can learn anything from? I had a sister who went through a series of five operations and eventually died. We all learned compassion and to show our love. And I don't think any of the 'ideal' families that we've seen on TV ever have had problems like that."

WHEN MY SON, ERIC, was about four, he had a cold one week and was confined to bed. He was keenly interested in cars and trucks at the time, and had seen an advertisement on television for a little motorized car that zoomed around on tracks; he was absolutely enchanted with this toy. Eric was a pretty reasonable boy, never one to hold me up for every toy he took a fancy to, and although he didn't press for this one, I knew he was desperate to have it. I brought it home from the store one evening and he was thrilled. I set up the tracks, installed the batteries, Eric pushed GO—and the little car limply moved along, nothing like the commercial that showed it racing across the floor and from one set of tracks to the other.

Eric said, "What's wrong with it, Dad?"

I said, "Well, maybe it's the batteries," so I ran out and got a fresh set of batteries. The car still hardly moved.

I brought our car and tracks back to the store and suggested that the set might be defective. The clerk told me I was the first person who had complained.

"I'm not really here to complain," I said. "I just want this thing to work—I've got a disappointed child."

I returned home with a new set and put in the new batteries. The car still didn't work the way it did on TV, to Eric's dismay and my annoyance. The following holiday season, Eric got some toys that he enjoyed very much. He said to me, "Dad, this doesn't get advertised on television. It really works." He had drawn a cause-and-effect relationship that made sense to him—if a toy was on TV, it must be no good.

We talked a bit about the differences we'd noticed between toys as they look in TV commercials and as they appear in real life. Eric had noticed that the "action figures" and other dolls we had seen on commercials are actually, in the store, tiny little things in enormous boxes. We talked about how the toy commercials are filmed and put together in such a way as to make the toys look a great deal more exciting and dynamic than they really are. I said, "The people who make these advertised toys don't care as much about your pleasure as they do about my money."

He said, "But that's not fair!"

And I said, "I agree with you, it's not fair."

Eric shook his young head in disgust.

The Television Set: Its Uses and Abuses

Our children are TV kids. They have grown up with the television set a fixture of their homes and their daily lives. And television is a seductive, compelling medium. You sit and watch it. You can't do anything to it; it does things to you. It gets messages through to you—some directly, some subtly and indirectly. And children, whose startling number of viewing hours have been well documented, absorb its steady barrage of commercial pitches, scenes of violence and damaging illusions about family relationships and society's values.

Participants in the Mellman & Lazarus survey were quite clear in their convictions that TV, while here to stay, was a presence they were not very happy about, especially when it comes to their children. While a majority of Americans, according to the survey, do not place primary blame for all our problems on the media, a small but significant number thought the influence of television and movies was one of the major causes of crime and other social problems. And nearly one-third of all participants believed that one effective way to strengthen family values would be through providing better images and role models on TV and in the movies.

They spoke with vehemence about their concerns. Said one, "I think we're confused because we get mixed messages in the media. We have sex and violence on TV, and yet they don't want to air a condom ad." Said another, "The difference between the real family and the TV family is that the TV family is already perfected. The situations and answers are already dealt with— whereas in real life, mistakes are made, the wrong thing is said and you have to learn from it."

TV programming, of course, is determined by what kinds of programs will deliver the largest number of bodies with wallets to the sponsoring companies, which usually turn out to be shows emphasizing violence, promiscuous sex, crime and other unacceptable behaviors. Conflict is what makes life-according-to-TV interesting and the only news is bad news. (As a former president of France once said, the media are not interested in the train that arrives in the station on time, but will go on endlessly about the train that crashes into the station.) Happy families are seen as boring. Superficial attractiveness and thrills are extolled. Blood, war and murder are right in our living rooms. News people stake out accident sites and the homes of bereaved families. Cartoon characters blow each other up. And children watch it all.

Obviously, TV is here to stay and there's nothing inherently bad about the medium or even about "parking" the children in front of the set occasionally, as long as parents monitor the programs their children watch, have rules about viewing time, make opportunities to talk with children about what they're seeing and make certain the set does not dominate the home. (I'm astonished at the number of families that have TV sets right in the middle of the living room, dining room or kitchen, sometimes playing all day and indiscriminately, so that conversation must be conducted around the TV. People watching TV tend not to make eye contact. Before television, in the humble days of radio, people could listen to the radio *and* look at each other.)

I do believe that children should be discouraged from watching violence on TV and should instead be encouraged to view programs of an informational or educational nature. And I'd be happy to see violence on TV eliminated altogether, for there are indications that children who view a great deal of it are indeed affected by it. Many observers have pointed out that the games children play seem more violent now, that they enjoy aggressive games and war toys. Certainly, television isn't the only place that children are exposed to excessive violence, and it is realistic to acknowledge also that children must learn to deal with hostility and aggressiveness. But exposure to excessive violence and the glorification of brutal actions that so often typifies TV fare can only serve to desensitize children and make them think that such behavior is permissible.

If your youngsters enjoy their Saturday morning cartoon "fix," take some time to watch the shows with them and see what's going on and how they react to antics that often include punching and hitting or bizarre scenes of characters being flattened by a speeding train and then popping back to life. In general, children older than five know that the slugging and battering that take place in some cartoons or adventure shows is extremely exaggerated and at times totally unrealistic. Children under the age of five, however, may see characters knocking each other about with no apparent harm and expect the same carefree consequences to result in real life if they imitate what they see. Actions in cartoons or slapstick comedies are viewed by young children in a literal and concrete way, and your children may need some help in learning to differentiate between fantasy and reality. Sit on the floor and watch for a bit with your child, and, when the occasion arises say, "It looks fun and silly, doesn't it, when that guy punches the other one and he goes sailing through the window and lands on his nose. But that's not something people can do in real life, you know."

Watch news shows together with older children and talk about and react to what you're hearing and seeing. Programs that deal with painful topics or news stories about wars or natural disasters can actually help sensitize children to human suffering and make them aware of the greater world and historical events. They can be helped to understand about the very real ravages of war and the fact that injustice and great cruelty occur in the world. But you should be with them, helping them to understand the feelings that are aroused. Talk about your own dismay that such things can happen. Make it clear that you are moved and deeply concerned about what you see and that everyone must do what he or she can to prevent bad things from happening in the world.

Small children who watch news reports or crime shows often do not understand that what they are seeing on television is not a random selection of life's events, but a distillation and condensation of the worst things happening on a given day. And youngsters who are perhaps more creative and more capable of speculating about the vagaries of life can sometimes be overstimulated by their own fantasies, fed by the real events they hear about on television, of what disaster might happen to them. In my years of work with children, I've heard many accounts of how "that bad man can find ways of getting into our house and coming to my room." In some cases, these fantasies are fears motivated by an underlying psychological problem, but perfectly sound and healthy children who happen to be bright or particularly imaginative may be easily overwhelmed by "what could happen."

If you sit by passively, viewing such programs without expressing sensitivity or outrage, your children may feel that you don't particularly care when human beings are hurt because they happen to live in oppressive countries or can be destroyed by natural disasters. Talk about TV commercials and how ads try to get us to buy something we probably don't really need—or that probably doesn't taste as good or work as well as we're being led to believe.

Commercials also sometimes send the message that nobody should feel anything but great pleasure. Ads for painkillers indicate that we are entitled not to suffer through a small headache and that two tablets or a spoonful of the advertised product will instantly enable us to implement that entitlement. Other ads urge people to get away and take a cruise—it's only three days, everybody is just relaxing and having fun, and, sure, you deserve it. These messages add up to something pretty powerful, even for children, who do not themselves buy medications or cruise tickets. They attempt to persuade us that life *should* be free of frustrations and that relief from frustrations is pretty easy to obtain—a message that can be damaging to children, who need to learn that some of the greatest satisfactions come through meeting difficult responsibilities and tackling adversity. And that a big task of growing up is developing the capacity to put off immediate gratification. Point out the reality that television is a business, and that advertising tends to highlight things in the best possible way. I told a friend the story about Eric and the little car that really didn't work very well, and she said, "In our household we've made it a rule that we never buy products that are advertised on television. So when we go to a store to buy things, we look for items that we've never seen in TV commercials." This way, she says, she's never harassed by demands for this particular toy or that cereal. You might tell your child that if a toy or cereal is really good, they don't need to advertise, because people will buy it anyway.

The media undeniably can promote positive values as well as negative ones. So many children now are concerned about the environment, for example, setting up recycling centers under the sink, rescuing soda cans from the street, largely because of the power of the media to broadcast this critical message. Getting news from the other end of the world in seconds, teaching millions of people about language, medicine and history, photographing planets from outer space are all stunning displays of the immediacy and range of the television medium. But we have to recognize its potential to undermine our most deeply held family values.

Limiting the amount of TV that your child watches isn't a bad idea, but a better solution is teaching him how to select programs and joining in the viewing experience, at least from time to time, sharing your observations and feelings, objecting to aggressive or rude behavior or foul language. There's certainly nothing wrong with unwinding with a bit of escapist entertainment now and then. We don't want people censoring what we see; neither can we stop programs from airing that are in poor taste or have a negative influence, because the television time is paid for by someone who wants to sell a product. But we can make our children aware that TV offers up an often distorted view, that the glamour and drama on the screen are not what we should expect or even want in our real lives, and that most families are not like the Cosbys *or* the Simpsons, et al. And that we don't allow certain ways of behaving or speaking in our homes, no matter what some TV people do.

Media Scares and a Child's Nightmares

One special focus of media attention in recent years I feel has had an unnecessarily upsetting, fear-provoking effect on young children. When a child, tragically, has been abducted or found killed, newspapers and news reports have been central in fomenting an atmosphere of panic that has left many children and parents worried out of all proportion to a real danger and vulnerable to hysterical efforts to "protect the children." Several years ago, a group of merchants organized a day during which children could be fingerprinted at shopping malls, the fingerprints to be useful for identification if the child was kidnapped. Their efforts received national publicity, and over a period of several weeks, I was asked to comment on television discussion shows and in newspaper editorials on this fingerprinting.

I acquired various statistics on missing children, including some from a professional organization for pathologists, which had begun to investigate the issue in response to the perceived public concern, with a view to teaching people how to identify bodies. But they found that the incidence was small, and that the majority of these unfortunate children had wandered off and met with accidents—they had not been abducted by murderous kidnappers, their bodies left unidentified.

Certainly, one missing or murdered child is an unspeakable tragedy. As parents, we find even imagining such a fate for our child too painful to dwell on. But it became clear that the urgings to bring all children in for fingerprinting, because then parents could feel safer with the realization that the children could be identified, was in large part a marketing gimmick to get people to shopping malls to spend their money. (Police officials, in fact, have insisted that footprints are actually more useful in identifying a child.) Over a period of five years, fewer than a thousand children have been taken nationwide, the great majority in divorce-custody disputes, by relatives.

I was appalled by these efforts, which upset parents. Parents were made anxious and left with the feeling that "I can't let my child walk out the door because someone is waiting to abduct him." In lectures I gave that touched on this subject, usually in response to parents' questions about how they might sufficiently warn their children about the dangers of kidnappers, I used a small demonstration to illustrate the actual statistical risk. We know figures on the number of people with AIDS. I would ask an audience of five hundred or a thousand people, "How many of you here know somebody with AIDS?" A reasonable percentage would raise their hands. Then I would ask, "How many people here know someone whose child has been abducted?" No one raised a hand.

A flurry of books and games has been published on how to get home safely, first, fastest. Missing children's faces have been printed on milk cartons and shopping bags. While every effort should be made to locate a missing child, every child should not be made fearful about the chances of his remaining safe the moment he leaves home. Many parents have told me that their children wake up terrified, dreaming that their picture was on a milk carton. A friend's daughter asked him over breakfast, "Would you put my picture on the milk box if I disappeared?"

In our urgency to inform our children about real dangers, we may be instilling feelings of fear more than promoting reasonable caution. I have strong feelings about the idea that children shouldn't talk to strangers. My daughter once came home from school saying that her teacher had talked to the class about how important it was not to talk to strangers. My daughter said to me, "But if you don't talk to strangers, how can you ever make friends?"

I said, "Pia, you're absolutely right," and I've adopted her point of view. I believe parents should encourage children to be friendly to strangers, with certain exceptions. A parent might say, "Don't talk to strangers who want you to get into a car or say they want you to go with them to help look for a lost kitten, or tell you that your Mom or Dad has sent them to get you. There are a few people who want to harm children. But most people, and most strangers who want to say hello to you or to talk, are just being friendly."

We need to teach our children how to deal with the hazard, but we also should explain that most strangers aren't a hazard. We need to give our children specific advice on how to deal with real dangers—not only how to cross the street, but what to do if a stranger exposes himself or makes threatening gestures—and at the same time, let them know that not everybody walking the streets is a dangerous person out to get a child. Reassure your child, if she worries about faces on milk cartons, that although these bad things do sometimes happen, you are looking out for her safety and you know she has learned the ways to keep herself safe.

War Toys and Fighting Games

Whenever I speak to groups of parents about their child-raising concerns, I am asked whether games and toys that have to do with battles, weapons, good guys and bad guys and conquering the enemy are dangerous influences for children. Parents who abhor fighting and violence wonder if they should flat-out forbid their children to play with toy guns or to have video games in which winning means destroying an opponent.

Most very young children, boys in particular, go through a phase of enjoying pretend "shooting" at other people or birds or planes. Most of them spontaneously pass out of this "shoot-'em-up" stage and become equally fascinated with other things as they get older and their range of interests increases. There is not much point in confiscating a youngster's toy gun; the child will use fingers or a stick as an imaginary gun, and a parent's prohibitive attitude will only make the activity more alluring. But a parent can convey values about violence in general and guns in particular.

If your youngster is spending a lot of time running around going "bang-bang" at everything in sight, you might tell him that you don't enjoy seeing him playing in this manner. Let him know that guns can hurt people badly, sometimes even kill them, and that you would like it if he had fun in other kinds of ways. By making your feelings and displeasure known—without overreacting to such an extent that the forbidden gunplay becomes even more desirable—you should get your message across.

When my son was five or six, a psychiatrist friend of mine brought him a toy gun for Christmas, a replica of a real rifle that even sounded real when it went off. I asked my friend privately, "Charlie, why did you do that?" He said, "Well, he's a boy, and he probably has to get rid of his aggressions."

I said, "I think you're being presumptuous."

My friend assumed that inside every boy are layers of hostility that have to be worked through, an assumption I didn't share. What bothered me more was that I couldn't forbid my son to play with this amazing rifle. It was a gift; it was his.

The following day I said to Eric, "It disturbs me to see toys like that. If you want to play with it, you may, but don't do it when I'm around. Please? It reminds me of war. It reminds me of people getting killed. I've seen people shot and killed and it's very upsetting, so that's why I feel this way about guns."

He said, "Okay, Dad."

I didn't restrict him or embarrass him; I transmitted my thoughts and values.

A few months later, we walked into a toy store not far from home on Saturday afternoon. Eric, who was marching ahead of me, stopped abruptly a few steps inside the door and said, "Dad, don't go any farther. Don't look over there. You'll get very, very unhappy." Of course, I had to look, and there was a rack of toy guns.

I was delighted because it told me that Eric understood, that he respected my feelings. And more: that I had successfully conveyed my values.

Getting and Giving at Holiday Time

The superficial, acquisitive, "more and bigger and better things" values promoted by media commercialism seem most pervasive and overweening around the Christmas holidays. Parents, frayed by their child's want-lists and the barrage of ever-more-high-pitched ads for the newest and latest toys and gadgets, find it especially difficult to convey values in this frenzied, festive atmosphere.

It helps to realize that a certain amount of greed is normal in young children, who are naturally self-centered. Two-year-olds, for example, will normally push, pull and grab, and have little concept of sharing. A child doesn't really want everything he sees; he does *want* this thing *now,* and during the height of the holiday advertising season, the number of must-have items seems vast. Children also are hearing friends who are *definitely* getting the hand-held video game with color or the doll townhouse, and may entertain fears of being left out and friendless if they do not keep pace with the very latest stuff.

It's never a good idea to rant about a child's "greediness" or make comparisons with your own, less-indulged childhood. It *is* a good idea to try honestly to appreciate your child's feelings. Say: "Look, I know you really want that. I know some of your friends will be getting it. I know you're suffering and I also know what that feels like, because it happened to me when I was a kid. But we can't afford that right now (or, that is not something I think you should have). It would be nice if things were different, but this is the way it is. And you'll do okay without it."

Make it clear that you understand how strong your child's feelings are about this particular item, and perhaps suggest alternative presents that *are* within your means or that you don't object to. The chances are he will still be disappointed when he ultimately realizes he's really not going to get the desired item, but he will remember that you told him the truth. And by telling him the truth, you are in a good position to help him deal with whatever emotional distress may occur at the time.

The whole hoopla leading up to the holidays provides a wonderful opportunity to talk to your children about this annual promotion of materialism, about the purpose of gift giving and about the real meaning of Christmas. I would also talk to very young children, right from the start, about the real meaning of Santa Claus, saying in so many words that Santa Claus is not a real creature who delivers gifts to good children, but an imaginary character that it's fun to pretend about.

While I dislike encouraging the idea of Santa-the-gift-giver, I very much favor perpetuating the *myth* of Santa. A myth is a story passed down from generation to generation, or as Webster's dictionary puts it, "A person or thing existing only in imagination." Children love and enjoy myths, and even at an early age can understand how they are different from reality. While I don't recommend stopping youngsters as they walk down the street and telling them that "Santa Claus is a fake," I do believe children should be told the truth about Santa when they ask if he is real.

I remember talking to my own children about Santa, the make-believe character, and describing how he came through the sky with reindeer and stopped at everybody's home. They had no trouble accepting this. One Christmas Eve when we were sitting around the fire near a big picture window, I looked out and said, "Pia, I think I see him coming!" We looked up into the sky together and she said, "Dad, I think I see him too!" And we both laughed. Even grown-ups like to pretend that Santa is real around Christmastime.

Children think it's pretty cool that Mom and Dad pretend Santa is real. And making it clear that you're just pretending together relieves you of the need to explain just how he gets into millions and millions of houses around the world and why he discriminates and visits only good children, not the "bad" children. A child who believes that a little white-haired man up north makes toys all year that he then gives, for free, to "good" children can easily conclude that the pile of gifts under the tree on Christmas is a clear indication that he himself has been good. Or that a poor child who didn't receive many gifts didn't deserve them because he was bad. Children have enough troubles without going through this sort of thought process.

Of course, the best way to counteract unhealthy, materialistic values is first to demonstrate good ones. Gifts don't have to be bought; they can be made. Encourage and help children to make gifts, baking cookies or cakes together or making things during summer vacations. Small children can collect pinecones or flower petals, make and decorate simple cloth bags to put them in and give them as gifts to be put out in a bowl or basket. When my children were little, I would encourage them to go to the five-and-ten and buy inexpensive frames that they could paint or decorate with simple stick-ons. They would put one of their own drawings or paintings in the frame, wrap it in their own way and give it to a family member or friend. These charming little gifts were always much appreciated, and some are still hanging in friends' homes.

Gifts shouldn't be given by rote. The parent who goes to the store, finds an item on sale and buys two dozen to "take care of" her gift list is modeling the wrong values for her child. When a grown-up does need to give gifts to many people, she can respect the uniqueness of each in some small way. Years ago, I gave small presents to the people who worked in my office, each of whom happened to like Dutch chocolates. My daughter and I would shop together for small boxes of chocolate, taking care to select a different kind for each person. Practicality can always be balanced with thoughtfulness, and children can learn that it's not necessary to spend a lot to be creative. Many of our friends who live in northern Maine can't afford to buy gifts, so each year they make pots of jam, an activity that's become a family tradition. And we have a pleasant memory of friends every time we spread the jam on our toast.

Unless we live in a cave, we're never far removed in our modern society from those insidious influences that pressure us to buy what we don't need, that try to tell us what to think and that can cause caring parents to feel at times the lesser empowering force in their children's lives. We only need to remember that the values that shape children's behaviors are almost always most powerfully conveyed within the family.

11
Tough
Times

"We've played yo-yo for these last twenty years. When things got tight, I went out and worked until it got comfortable, and then I'd stay home with the children. And then when things got tight again, I'd go back to work."

I WAS ABOUT EIGHT years old when my father lost his job during the Depression, just as my oldest brother was about to enter medical school. I vividly remember my parents' fierce determination that this setback would not be allowed to interfere with my brother's schooling and, in particular, my mother's stern voice saying, "If I have to scrub floors or take in boarders, that's what I will do. We won't let anything get in the way of school." In the midst of an emotionally trying time, when, as any youngster would, I felt unsettled and disturbed by family circumstances I was too young to fully understand, I found my mother's reaction comforting and reassuring. She acknowledged that we had a problem, affirmed her conviction that education was important and that her children's needs were to be protected, and indicated that she was determined to do whatever was necessary to get us through this time.

We all contributed ideas about what we could do to live within our reduced means. Over the months to come my own part in the family's effort included wearing some outdated hand-me-down clothes (I was in knickers when all my classmates had long pants), being careful not to waste food and entertaining myself not with new toys but by reading and visiting the museum or playing in the park. I was not always happy about this enforced austerity, but neither did I question its necessity or feel any truly deep-seated sense of loss. And in retrospect, I can see that the way my family dealt with this adversity had a strong effect on my own sense of family and my respect for education. I also learned early on that having money or the things it buys has little to do with feelings of self-esteem.

Tough times—when a father or mother loses a job, when a parent or close family member becomes ill or dies—can make family connections more critical than ever. Perhaps at no time since the Depression have so many American families experienced economic difficulties and the uncertainties of a shifting and, in some ways, dwindling job market.

According to the Mellman & Lazarus survey, while the vast majority of Americans find their families are the source of their greatest pleasure and joy in life, more than half also say that taking care of their families and providing financial security for themselves and those who depend on them is one of the things they worry about most, and they are deeply concerned about what the future holds. Said one man with two young children, "I worry about providing for them and making sure they have a good life, what they'll be like when they reach my age, and what the world will be like."

So many parents feel overwhelmed. The circumstances of our lives are changing so fast, and what worked for our parents often doesn't work for us. Few of us can choose to take care of our children full time. Housing costs are high and a new generation of young couples faces the real possibility of never being able to own a home. Many jobs aren't secure and some of us must hold more than one job. Over half the women with preschool-age children are working or looking for work, compared to just 12 percent in 1950. And in a time when the extended family is so often splintered, when so many young families and old people are isolated from each other, the inevitable crises of life—illness, death, emotional struggles—are harder to get through. And parenting can be especially tricky—do we tell the children what's going on? How do we help them handle grief or anger or worry?

Many of us who are parents remember the parenting model of our own childhoods, when the youngsters were told as little as possible about the family's problems and grown-ups' concerns. Children needed to be protected, it was thought, from all those grown-up worries or their feelings of security will be damaged. Chances are we probably also remember that that approach didn't work. The tension in the air between a mother and father, strained conversations or painful silences, worried looks, quiet or angry talks behind closed doors—all were palpable, disquieting signs that something was wrong, something was going on, and we weren't being told. And, probably, in the absence of information to the contrary, we suspected that something *we* had done was to blame for the unhappy atmosphere in the home.

I am convinced that tough times can be among the best times to instill and strengthen in children two of the family values we consider most important: being responsible for one's actions, and providing emotional support to one's family. We know now that sharing unpleasant situations with children doesn't make them insecure or especially fearful and that, in fact, protecting children from problems and sorrows can actually do real damage. I once counseled a woman in her late twenties who suffered from severe hay fever and a terrible panic about traveling. At one point in our talks, Melissa told me about her father, who had died the summer she turned twelve. In an effort to shield Melissa from this terrible loss, her mother immediately sent her off to camp. The child didn't attend the funeral, didn't take part in the family's grieving, and never really had a chance to cry.

The unconscious has a strange way of dealing with such experiences. In the process of psychotherapy, it became clear to both of us that the tears she'd held inside had been trickling out during hay fever season. Her fear of travel, we discovered, related directly to the fact that she had been sent away and had then returned from camp that long-ago summer to face the shock and the grief that her father was not there. Travel became the equivalent of facing the reality of her father's death. When Melissa was able to reexperience that grief and cry over the loss of her father fifteen years earlier, there was a dramatic improvement in her symptoms.

Children need to learn to deal with adversity. When they face difficult realities, they begin to develop critical skills for getting through life. And a parent who is honest with her child, even about the minor adversities of real life—who says, for example, before a trip to the doctor, "We've got to go to the doctor; she's going to give you an injection and it's going to hurt a little—you can hold my hand if you want," is helping him learn to master the discomforts and pain he will inevitably repeatedly have to face.

Certainly, parents shouldn't share every gory detail about a family setback or convey information or feelings about financial problems or other losses that will burden the child with overwhelming feelings of helplessness. But our children are family members, and part of being a family is sharing in responsibility. When a parent explains instead of evades, the child begins to hone his own mechanisms for dealing with difficult issues. When children have questions about things and we distort the truth, even out of love, they conjure up their own answers. And often those answers are pretty far from reality.

When Money Is Tight

A parent's job loss and the subsequent need to cut back on spending is always a tough family issue, one that can produce feelings of fear and anger and uncertainty. Children need to be aware of what the family is going through and take part in finding ways to get through. When parents attempt to hide the fact that the family is facing financial problems, a child, who will almost certainly become conscious of those problems, may end up with the notion that there's something shameful about the situation, that people with more money are "better than we are."

I don't think parents need to be resolutely cheerful or unnaturally optimistic. Hiding all negative emotions isn't a good lesson either, and there's nothing wrong with admitting that you're not very happy about the situation, that you're looking forward to the time when things will be better and that some of the adjustments everyone will have to make will be unpleasant. What's important is to avoid creating the feeling that there are no options, that there's nothing anyone can do. Children need to feel their parents are in control and are capable of formulating plans to keep the family secure.

Some families regularly have "family meetings" to talk about any issues affecting them, discuss problems or differences of opinion, give children an opportunity to participate in making choices about what furniture to buy or where to take a vacation. Those families will probably find such a getting together the ideal way to talk about the fact that Dad lost his job or Mom is going to be going back to work and we're all going to have to make some difficult changes. I don't think it's a particularly good idea, however, to summon everyone for such a conference if the family has not been in the habit of holding regular meetings of this nature. The formal sit-down discussion might seem a bit alarming and give children a sense of imminent doom. A casual, informal talk that gets across the facts and the main points of change for the child's life—"Dad's job was ended and he's going to be working at home setting up a business here" or "Mom is going to be working two nights a week"—will convey the feeling that what has happened is not particularly out of the ordinary and that Mom and Dad are taking actions to resolve the problem.

Children will often have questions, which should be encouraged, and small children in particular may express basic fears about not having enough food to eat or not having a place to live. It's helpful to a child if his parent is calmly reassuring and quite specific in her answers—"We'll have plenty of food to eat but we won't be going to restaurants for a while and we won't be buying some kinds of things we like but don't really need." While children need to know what changes the family will be going through, they don't need to be burdened with larger issues they may not even be thinking of. It's a good idea to answer a child's questions honestly but not introduce ones he hasn't raised.

Older children, who are keenly aware of their friends' lives and who get a lot of their satisfaction and feelings of self-worth from fitting into the peer group, can feel crushed by a change in the family's financial status. They may be embarrassed about a parent's unemployment, angry or hurt at not being able to have the latest fashion in sneakers or to go on the class trip out of town. Those feelings should be acknowledged. It *isn't fun* to miss out on things or to feel different from everyone else. Let the child vent his feelings. Don't accuse him of being thoughtless or self-absorbed. Admit that what he's going through is not much fun.

These times are a wonderful opportunity to talk about values. Explain to your child that being out of work is nothing to be embarrassed about—it happens at some time or other to most people. Tell your child that she doesn't need to give excuses or elaborate explanations to her friends—only a brief statement that her dad is job hunting and that she won't have money to do some things for a while. Help your child understand that having less money doesn't mean he deserves less respect, nor is it anything to be ashamed of. Use examples from your own experience to help him see that being a happy and caring individual doesn't depend on wealth or material possessions. And tell him that he will get through this uncomfortable time and not be much the worse for wear.

Most parents, in fact, are surprised at just how sympathetic, caring and helpful their children turn out to be during times when the family is financially strapped. I think it's a marvelous idea and an opportunity for growth to solicit suggestions from everyone on how the family's expenses can be minimized. Teenagers might suggest taking on an after-school job or contributing to the family some of their earned money. Younger children might be intensely involved in going over the weekly grocery list and coming up with ways to cut back, such as making cookies at home instead of buying packaged ones.

All children at some point will desperately *have* to have a particular toy or item of clothing. If the budget really will not allow for the child's getting the hotly desired object, his parents should at least recognize that his unhappiness is real and serious. Try saying something like, "I really wish I could give you what you want, but it's impossible right now. I know it makes you unhappy, and it also makes me unhappy for you not to have what you want." Then offer to do something together that you can afford—a picnic, a bike ride, something that will be fun. The child will survive his disappointment.

It's painful for parents to be compelled to deny their children things and to watch them having to wrestle with some of the realities of economic hard times, just as the loss of a job and income is a wrenching worry. But living through these times together generally has a unifying effect in families where emotional support and mutual respect are solid values, and most people tend to look back at these periods with a real appreciation of how much they gained.

When Illness or Death Strikes the Family

Family and friends are never more important than during times of illness and death. All the rituals that guide our behavior—from the simple practice of sending flowers to someone in the hospital, to the ancient formal routines of the funeral, the wake or the shiva—give us a sense of reassurance, demonstrate our concern for the pain or grief of another person and help us work through our own grieving. Friends and family also help during the sometimes extended period of mourning, after the rituals surrounding death are over, when the turmoil and grief surrounding the loss of a loved one can lead to a desire for isolation, the feeling: "I don't want to be near anyone. I don't want to go through anything like this again. I don't have the strength to care for anyone again." I know from experience how vital it is at such times to have family and friends nearby, to give support and the reassurance that things will eventually change.

During my illness, when I was literally sedated for weeks on end, unable to communicate, my wife, Mary Jane, spent twenty-four hours a day focused on my needs. It was often difficult for her and my daughter to have decent meals, since they spent so much time at the hospital. One evening a neighbor called Mary Jane and asked if there was anything she could do for her and Pia. Before my wife could answer, the neighbor said, "I think I'll bring you something to eat." The next morning she came by with roasted chickens and all kinds of goodies. Many friends sent notes, books, little tokens of concern during my long recuperation, and when I thanked them, many said, "I remember when I was ill and someone brought a little gadget or game that took my mind off things. I thought you might need something like that right now." And one day, much later, my lawyer and friend called to say, "I'd be glad to come over a few days this week and help you sort out your office and all the mail that's piled up during your illness. You don't even have to move. I'll hold things up and you can tell me where to put them."

What wonderful displays of emotional support these well-thought-out, simple but useful caring kinds of help are, reflecting the ability to translate some of our experiences with adversity into loving behavior that we demonstrate toward others. How good it feels, too, to be the giver. And what an important opportunity to model values for our children.

To a young child, a grown-up's illness is a scary thing. All children are fearful of losing parents, and if a parent is ill, they may see the illness as something that will take the parent away. Some children may become overprotective, hovering close by and showing real signs of their fear of loss. Others may deal with their anxiety by denying the illness, with the unconscious idea that if I don't react to Mom as if she's sick, then she's not. Children can be helped to accept the idea that a parent is ill if they're reminded that sometimes they've been sick too, and they needed someone to take care of them until they were well again.

But death is a concept the young child really cannot understand, certainly not before someone he knows well—a relative, a pet, a neighbor—someone who has "been there" suddenly isn't there anymore. Most children at that point will have a lot of questions to ask: "Where did Grandfather go when he got dead?" "When will he come back?" "Why didn't the doctor fix him?" "When will you die?" "When will I die?" These are awfully hard questions for a parent to answer, especially if the answers seem to be making the child more anxious, and it's perfectly natural to wish to avoid them, give rushed or diluted answers and to feel uncomfortable.

Again, it's best to give honest answers to specific questions and to avoid answering questions that have not been asked or give answers that stretch the child's capacity to understand. You might say, "Grandpa has just stopped living and he can't be fixed again. He won't be able to do the things he used to do and we won't see him." Tell the child that you are sad and unhappy about this, and that you're going to miss Grandpa a lot. It's perfectly all right, if you feel it, to cry a little or express your own grief in some such way. Children need to understand grief. If your child sees you grieve, he is helped to value life.

Certainly, never refer to death as "going to sleep for a long time." A child who's been led to believe that dying is somehow like sleeping understandably begins to fear going to sleep at night or may have nightmares. Or he worries that when Mom and Dad go to sleep they're never coming back, which is a real fear of all young children. If your child asks, "When will you die?" or "Am I going to die?" I think it's a good idea to say something like, "I won't die for a long, long, long, long time," drawing out all the "longs" to give your child the idea that nobody is going to die soon. You can't deny that you will die or that your child will die, and you should know that your child is going to think about death a lot no matter what answers you give, but you can convince him in his own terms that all this is a very, very, very, very long time in the future.

Experiencing "moderate" amounts of grief is psychologically valuable for a child. Like Melissa, who was shielded from the direct experience of her father's death, children who are not allowed to participate in some way in the mourning for a loved one often develop fantasies or symptoms that are far more upsetting than the actual experience would have been. I think children should attend funerals, if the dead person was an immediate family member and if the child will not be subjected to an open coffin or the actual burial. Appropriate participation in a family's expression of grief and loss really makes a child feel better about what has happened than if he's excluded or if those around him show no signs of grief at all.

A parent's death, of course, is a searing loss to a child of any age, and there is, realistically, no way to reduce the child's trauma. The child may feel desperately sad, or guilty because of thoughts he was somehow responsible for his parent's death, or angry because of the perception that his all-powerful parent must have chosen to die and leave him. These are terribly upsetting feelings for the surviving parent who is going through her own grieving. I think it's best to tell a child that it will take a long time to get over his unhappy feelings and that in a way he will never completely stop feeling sad and missing that person. The child should also be told that no one will ever really be able to replace his missing parent. The child's feelings should be acknowledged, he should be encouraged to talk about those feelings, and he should be given an abundance of love and reassurance.

Facing life's problems head-on and developing the skills for coping are far better for children in the long run than being protected from harsh realities. But when a family is under stress, its members need to extend to each other—and get from others, from relatives and from that extended community of people who make you feel important in their lives—extra measures of love, respect and emotional support.

12
Human
Resources:
Family Values in Child Care, in the Workplace

"When I was growing up, it wasn't just the parents. We more or less had a community of people who cared for you and looked out for you, which inspired you."

ACCORDING TO the Mellman & Lazarus study, Americans desperately want to find ways to spend more time with their families. And faced by economic pressures that in many families compel both parents to work, by social changes that limit the options for how children can be cared for during the day, clearly many families feel they are swimming upstream. As never before in our history, perhaps, families need real support from communities, government and businesses.

Family Values on the Job

A now-classic study in human relations took place in the late 1920s at Western Electric's Hawthorne plant near Chicago. One of its findings came to be called the Hawthorne Effect. Researchers went into the factory to see if by improving illumination for a group of employees productivity would increase. Improvements did indeed seem to boost worker output. But much to their surprise, when the researchers analyzed a comparable group with no change in illumination, the productivity also increased. Further study and analysis of this puzzling result showed that productivity increased because the workers were delighted that management was showing some kind of interest in them. They felt valued.

Employers who reach out, who are responsive to employees and their needs as individuals and family members, can be part of a new, broader definition of family. Most people are willing to define coworkers in the workplace as family, if they find closeness, support, mutual respect and shared values. And people do things for family that they won't do for others. Turnover, loyalty, absenteeism and productivity can all be influenced by employers who are willing to share their employees' family concerns. You could say that every CEO is potentially a parent to all of his company's employees.

I once tried to get the CEO of a company I was consulting with to establish a policy that every employee would be expected to leave work to attend his or her child's school plays and other significant daytime events in the child's life. The message given would be, "We really care about your children and your family life." I suggested to him that the public relations impact would be significant, always a persuasive argument, and said I'd be glad to appear on network television morning programs with the CEO to say "Here's a company that's leading the way. They truly believe that their employees and their families are important; they are giving them this time and expecting them to use it."

The CEO very much liked the idea, but as it wended its way through the organization to the people who would be responsible, it met with opposition. "Our employees can do these things whenever they want," was the feeling. "They have personal leave time they can use to go to school events if they want."

I said, "That's not the same message at all."

The final verdict was, "We don't think we can do this because it might lead to other problems and we're not so sure we're ready for them. People may take advantage of this and we'd have no way of checking on how they're using the time." It's not at all unusual, of course, for some large companies to publicly preach about their concern for their workers or to mount expensive advertising campaigns around vacant, sentimental claims of their concern for families and "American" values purely as a public relations gimmick. At these corporations, policy changes that would demonstrate that concern in real ways are rarely, if ever, implemented.

Over the next decade, two-thirds of new available workers will be women, most of childbearing age. It makes sense, including business sense, for employers to find ways to accommodate these workers' needs. Rigid schedules and procedures may be more a matter of tradition than of practicality. What stands in the way of flexible work hours? Why can't two people share a job? Why not allow workers voluntarily to reduce their work hours and pay for a few months during a family crisis, retaining prorated benefits and seniority?

The idea that work is work and families are families is an increasingly artificial and pointless separation. It's good for children to see what their parents do, and good for a parent to show off a child at work. I remember as a child going to visit the factory where my father worked. All the women who worked at the machines would come and pinch my cheeks and say, "Oh, isn't he cute! Look at his curly hair!" as my father introduced me as "the baby," the youngest of his three children. (When I was in my thirties, he was still introducing me as the baby.)

My father had a great sense of pride in his children, and as a father myself, I feel the same way. I frequently had my children visit me at work. I would pick them up during their nursery school days and bring them to have lunch with me at the hospital. Sometimes they would play in my office. I'd take them around and show them the labs and other points of interest.

I have a picture of my son taken at my former office when he was very young. He always wanted to wear a white coat like his dad. A secretary dressed him in a white coat, rolled up the sleeves and pinned up the hem, and we made a "doctor's" name tag for him. It's a funny picture, because he wears a real white coat today, which I never would have expected. Eric is now a six-foot-tall doctor; he used to play in the biochemistry laboratories in which he now studies. He remembers these people who are now his professors from the perspective of a little child. He feels "I've been here all my life. I know this place."

Work is such an important part of our lives. It's wonderful if a child understands that and gets to know the people her parents work with. Bringing your child to your place of work from time to time lets her see what you do for a living; it models the reality that grown-ups need to work and that it's a responsibility to be taken seriously. A visiting child loves to try out sitting at Mom's desk and using her computer at her office, or having a tour of Dad's shop and meeting the people he works with. When a friend brought her young daughter to spend half a day at Mom's office, the little girl was amazed to see that the bulletin board behind her mom's desk was covered with her own paintings and drawings. As her mother's coworkers came in and out in the course of the morning, several commented on the colorful artwork. One said she only wished she had some wallpaper that matched a particular drawing of purple grapes and green leaves. The youngster was speechless with embarrassed pride, and at home that night, spent hours making a copy for her Mom's friend—"not big enough to cover a whole wall," she said, "but maybe she can put it in a frame and pretend it's wallpaper."

It means so much to a child to feel connected to that part of his parents' life, to carry with him a mental picture of the place where his mom and dad work, to meet some of the people who share that time and place with his parents. Americans say their coworkers feel like family, some even closer than many real family members. All benefit when employers recognize that workers' first priorities are as parents and sons and daughters and make those allowances that help them assume their family responsibilities.

Child Care That Works

I recently spent several months visiting day-care facilities across the country as part of a project that engaged me. My observations constituted not a systematic piece of research, but a personal evaluation, and in the course of my visits I spoke to hundreds of parents, day-care workers and children. I spent time in relatively small facilities and in some "chains" that took in several hundred children a day.

I cannot overemphasize how upset I was when I returned. These children were in awful situations, and often the parents had no clue as to what their children's day was like. The children were bored, usually engaged in activities that were basically busywork. Little attempt was made to respond to them as individuals. They couldn't explore. No one was available to answer their questions or give them the kind of adult attention that helps a child get involved in things he's curious about. They were simply kept occupied until their parents returned to pick them up.

If people are clamoring for more and more day care of this sort, we will surely end up with a generation of unmotivated children. Studies of children and animals who are nurtured and responded to during early, critical periods of their lives show that later on they will take on even the most difficult challenges without giving up. When children reach out and attempt to get their caretakers to respond and nothing happens, the youngsters learn there's little point in trying to make connections or to go after things. They stop trying. This learned helplessness is a very real precursor of depression.

I found one facility in my tour of day-care centers that was working. Selection Research, Inc. (SRI), in Lincoln, Nebraska, has operated a nonprofit center in their own facility for ten years. From my point of view, their center is nearly ideal.

SRI is in the business of selecting people with talents. They have worked in the field of education for thirty years, studying what makes outstanding teachers, and have used their own proven techniques and interview system to find workers for their SRI Child Development Center. It shows. The center is administered by individuals with advanced degrees in early child development, who in turn hire caretakers, whom they refer to as "teachers," to work with individual groups of children. *All* employees demonstrate a wonderfully warm, loving spirit and real concern for children. In the way they hold the children, talk to them and encourage them, it's immediately apparent that the job is not a stepping stone to something else. They want to be right where they are.

At SRI, it's understood that employees bring their family concerns to work, because their children are cared for *at work,*

right near Mom's or Dad's office. Teachers, parents and children
are all on a first-name basis, and special events each month bring
everybody together. These teachers visit the families at home.
Parents who must go out of town sometimes ask their child's
teacher to stay with the child, and the teachers are usually delighted to help. Teachers keep a notebook on each child to record
what he has accomplished during the day, noting what they have
discovered about the child that's unique, what he loves to do or
worries about. They plan special activities that relate to the child's
special nature and needs. When parents pick up their children
after work, they read through the notebook, ask questions or
make suggestions if they wish, work with the teacher to set goals
and to ensure that each week, the child has a successful experience
recorded—often with photos that illustrate, for example, how one
youngster finished a painting project or another helped set up the
table for snacks.

It's wonderful to go through the center and watch a teacher
working with a child who's deeply entranced by a particular activity. A little girl who is fascinated by scientific-type explorations
is being encouraged to experiment with the properties of water
and volume, filling different-sized containers with water and sand.
She is not being required to paint, as some other children are
doing, or to sit in the reading corner. Individual interests are
nourished; manners and respect for others' interests are stressed.
And parents are encouraged to continue with those same activities
at home and to add their own observations to the child's notebook—all of which helps bridge the gap between the home and the
center. The focus is on maintaining the rhythm of family ties.

At the center, the children show the kind of curiosity and
excitement so painfully absent at most day-care facilities. We
spent several days shooting a videotape, and the children were
very eager to learn what we were doing. They clustered around,
asking dozens of questions. We showed them the equipment, let
them look through the camera lens and listen through the head-
phones. After their curiosity about these goings-on had been thoroughly satisfied, they paid no attention to us while we were
actually filming because they were so engaged in their own activities, their Montessori materials and special individual projects.
When we finished the taping and left, even the video crew really
missed those lively, interested children.

The center is set up with respect for all the things that are important to children. The youngsters are kept together in small, stable "family" groups. As they get older, they graduate to the next level together, and their teachers move with them. Because there is this continuity, the children don't experience the constant disruption of relationships so common in day care, where workers frequently are let go or quit, preventing the children from getting close to anyone. Half the SRI teachers have been with the center for over four years. All receive tangible evidence of respect. Incentive programs compensate teachers with bonuses, and the parents conduct fund-raisers to supplement the teachers' pay. SRI nominates a "teacher of the month," who is given an award and commended before a large audience.

Parents come over from their offices to visit their children and children can visit their parents. In fact, parents are *expected* to visit the center during the day, to have their lunchtime or their breaks with the children. In the infant program, mothers can continue breast-feeding if they wish, or come by to hold and play with their babies during the day. Children can talk to their parents on the phone, and a teacher may bring a youngster over for a little visit at Mom or Dad's office.

Once, when I was strolling through the SRI offices, I saw a mother working with her child beside her. I said, "It looks to me like you've got a good assistant." The mother said, "Oh yes, he helps me all the time. He loves being here working with me." And nobody raises questions or doubts. The corporate philosophy focuses not on work hours clocked but on work accomplished.

Child Care for the Future

Dr. Donald Clifton, the chairman of Selection Research, Inc., says, "Our company is built around the importance of human resources, the importance of people. And if you really believe in that, you have to express those beliefs toward children, because that's where the resource begins to develop. Otherwise, it's like being in the lumber business and not planting trees.

"If a company is interested in the best environment for its people, one in which they can grow and develop, it must think about how they feel when they're at work. And above all, they need an environment where they feel all right about their children, where their children are accessible, where they get the best care available. It makes a huge difference in workers' morale and in their productivity. There's no question that the parents of children who are cared for in the center miss less work because they are near their children and confident that they are taken care of."

It is appalling that the United States is one of the few developed countries in the world without an adequate child-care system. Individual companies must take up the slack by, among other things, establishing caring, on-site child-care centers that permit parents and children to interact during the work day. Nothing strengthens families like giving them more time together, and if corporations mandate that parents with children spend some part of their work time with them, children will not feel alienated and parents will feel like full participants in their children's daytime lives.

I am not aware of many franchised day-care centers that are successfully meeting the needs of their young charges. These centers often have cute buildings and attractive equipment, but the heart of such an institution is the staff, and when a day-care center is first and foremost a business that keeps costs low by underpaying workers or hiring workers with no particular gift for the work but an inability to find employment elsewhere, the heart will be missing. Child-care workers desperately need not only decent pay, but recognition for the vital work they're doing. The caregivers, teachers, social workers and others who provide support, affection and stability in children's lives, who help create loving, socially useful individuals, are the less-visible heroes of the family. Low pay and little recognition account for the horrendous turnover in most day-care centers, a devastating occurrence for the children, who need stability in their early relationships.

Apart from the fact that paying attention to family needs through appropriate child care is the right and human thing to do, it makes enormous sense from a business point of view. Corporations that have made a firm commitment to the family priorities of their workers, including Selection Research, Inc., and the Scandinavian Airline System, among increasing numbers of others, can attest to the fact that it pays off in dollars and cents. Turnover is low, productivity is high, because parents and children are near each other and Mom or Dad is not distracted by wondering what their child is doing and whether she's happily busy or idle and sadly passing the time until one of her parents arrives. The cost of an on-site program is comparable to that of an independent day-care center. And it is possible to find people with the talent and desire to work with young children who will forego higher-paying jobs for the pleasure and deep satisfaction of working in an environment that accords them respect and recognition.

I'd like to see every company head declare that each employee *must* go to school when a child is performing in a pageant or take half a day off when there is a birthday in the family. Or say, "An employee can bring, at company expense, his spouse and child along on every sixth trip he makes on company business." And allow parents special paid sick leave to care for sick children. Most parents have faced the upsetting juggling act of arranging to care for a sick child, and many remember, as I do, the comforting, important feeling we had as children when illness kept us home from school and our mothers propped us up in bed with coloring books and perhaps a favorite treat to eat. Industry has no choice, really, but to respond to the needs of parents who have sick children or older relatives who need help. The unmistakable message—"We are about you and your family; we are prepared to help you spend more time together"—surely puts that employer in the strongest position to attract and keep committed workers. Applying family values to the workplace does pay.

Industry is gradually learning the value of acknowledging family needs. More and more American corporations are providing some kind of child care, in addition to "elder-care" programs for workers with older parents, adoption counseling and benefits, professional guidance for workers whose children are experiencing school difficulties, and other innovative kinds of attention. More and more are demonstrating a willingness to consider flexible hours and work schedules, job sharing, family crisis leave time, and other measures of real support. Certainly, these changes have resulted from the increasing number of two-parent families in the work force and from the slow but eventual recognition that business has played a part in shortchanging our young people and weakening the family as a functioning unit in the process. Most companies that have instituted programs that assist families have done the right thing for the wrong reason. Understandably, they are concerned about the bottom line and have found that there are immense economic and productivity benefits that come from having workers with more peace of mind about their families. That's a critical lesson learned.

Future Directions

Lest we have lost sight of the changes that have occurred in our country in the last fifty years, we simply have to contemplate the following data supplied by the Fullerton, California, Police Department and the California Department of Education:

The top seven school problems in the 1940s:
1. Talking out of turn
2. Chewing gum
3. Making noise
4. Running in the halls
5. Cutting in in line
6. Dress code violations
7. Littering

The top seven school problems in the 1980s:
1. Drug abuse
2. Alcohol abuse
3. Pregnancy
4. Suicide
5. Rape
6. Robbery
7. Assault

Study after study and survey after survey show that Americans are overwhelmingly concerned about the quality of family life. The media are full of reports that we long to be close to our families—however they are constituted—that we are willing to fight for our families and that we agree that our greatest problems as a society have their origins in not meeting family needs.

There is not a mental health professional or sociologist who does not recognize that the destructive behavior, the violence and crime that plagues us as a nation, with drugs, alcohol abuse and the alienation of our youth, is directly related to the way we have been raised and to what did or did not happen in the early years of our lives.

Bringing more and more children into the world who have less and less opportunity to be nurtured with love or cultivated to respect one another, who have little self-respect and even less motivation to want to take on responsibilities to make this a better world, will simply increase the burdens we now face and will eventually weaken our capacity to survive as a civilization.

If our children and youth continue to experience neglect and are assaulted by environmental abuses of all kinds, including parents who do not have time to be with them, schools that are inadequate to teach them and families that are too weak to guide them toward a sense of morality that fosters respect for others, a commitment to responsibility and a capacity to love, we will not be able to halt the momentum of destructiveness we see today.

Parental leave bills are an important step in the direction of emphasizing the significance of families to industry, management and government. These early efforts are like blazing a trail through the wilderness. They may not necessarily be totally effective for dealing with the major aspects of family life, but the trail may be the beginning of a superhighway, a more substantial and effective policy to strengthen the family in America. A thousand-dollar tax credit for each child, for example, is a step in the right direction and a declaration that children are valuable. But our society must do much more to demonstrate that meeting the needs of children during crucial and critical early stages of development is a major investment in our future. The cost to society of children whose lives have been damaged by poor nutrition, poor educational opportunities, poverty and poor health management is devastating. Ignoring these problems in the face of all the knowledge we have about the factors that contribute to their causes is beyond belief when we think of the resources, power and supposed wisdom of our elected officials.

But while we need support from our institutions to make it

possible for us to be together and to function well as families, it is individual effort that is most critical. We have become lazy, and desensitized to the importance of love, respect and responsibility. We have surrendered our willingness to live by moral values. Unless we can consciously and assertively begin to treat others, especially those in our family, with the respect we demand for ourselves, we will have to face the continuation of the degenerative trend in our relations with one another.

Even with ideal arrangements in the workplace and strong government support in policies concerning the family, ultimately it remains to each of us to pick up our own "litter," to speak respectfully to one another, to exhibit compassion and understanding, to embrace a value system that will show our children that there are words and deeds that are not acceptable, and that each man and woman and child among us deserves respect.

Index